D1188334

MODEL RAILROADING

Gil Paust

MODEL RAILROADING

*How to Plan, Build, and Maintain
Your Trains and Pikes*

DOUBLEDAY & COMPANY, INC.
GARDEN CITY, NEW YORK

625.19

Library of Congress Cataloging in Publication Data

Paust, Gil.
Model Railroading.

Bibliography: p. 139.
Includes index.
1. Railroads—Models. I. Title.
TF197.P38   625.1'9
ISBN: 0-385-13033-3 Trade
ISBN: 0-385-13034-1 Prebound
Library of Congress Catalog Card Number 80–1817

To my wife, Anne,
for adding the romantic lore of the railroad
to its technology

ACKNOWLEDGMENTS

I AM DOUBLY INDEBTED to the editors of *Yankee Magazine* for their articles in their January issues of 1967, 1977, and 1980. They not only kept me informed that the love of railroadiana is alive and well and bustin' out all over with increasing fervor; they also led me to Adolph Arnold of Sharon, Massachusetts. Enriching this book are Mr. Arnold's photographs from his internationally famous railroad collection which he has been amassing for over two decades from all over the world, and which are now housed in his new, expanded A & D Toy-Train Village and Railway Museum in South Carver, Massachusetts.

Providing the expertise of a railroad executive as well as technical assistance in all aspects of the model railroading hobby was Tom Burns of Elmsford, New York, who knows more about model railroads than anyone I know.

A model railroader's best friends will be the staffs of his local hobby shops—mine are the staffs of America's Hobby Center in New York City and Roundhouse II in White Plains, New York. Invaluable aids are the meticulous catalogs of all the leading manufacturers I have listed at the end of this book. I am especially grateful to the personnel of Bachmann Brothers, Tyco Industries, and Model Power, for supplying me with photographs of some of their outstanding models, and to the executives of Floquil-Polly S Color Corp. for permission to reproduce illustrations from their booklet *Painting Miniatures,* which appear in chapter 9. My particular endorsement, also, goes to *Model Railroader* magazine—this monthly publication supplies experienced modelers as well as beginners with all the latest information on new developments and trends in the hobby.

CONTENTS

PREFACE   *Why Build a Model Railroad?*   1

VOCABULARY FOR MODEL RAILROADERS   5

SECTION I   THE WORLD OF MODEL TRAINS

1. BIRTH OF THE TRAIN HOBBY   13
2. MODEL RAILROADS TODAY   19

SECTION II   YOUR FIRST TRAIN

3. ADVANTAGES OF THE TRAIN SET   29
4. THE STORY OF LOCOMOTIVES   35
5. ROLLING STOCK   42
6. DO-IT-YOURSELF KITS   46
7. THE TRACKS   51
8. ARCHITECTURE   61
9. PAINTING AND DECORATING   66
10. LANDSCAPING   71

SECTION III   PLANNING YOUR PIKE

11. YOUR TRACK LAYOUT   83
12. POWER FOR YOUR PIKE   90
13. PIKE ACCESSORIES   101
14. MAINTENANCE   108

SECTION IV YOUR RAILROAD EMPIRE

15. PERFECTING YOUR PIKE 117
16. HIGHBALLING INTO THE FUTURE 125
17. TIPS, TRICKS, AND GIMMICKS 130

MY SOURCES OF MATERIALS AND
    INFORMATION

I. MANUFACTURERS AND
    THEIR SPECIALTIES 137

II. ASSOCIATIONS 139

III. MONTHLY MAGAZINES 139

IV. BIBLIOGRAPHY 139

INDEX 141

MODEL RAILROADING

PREFACE
Why Build
a Model Railroad?

THE RAILROAD ENGINE APPEARED IN AMERICA over a hundred and fifty years ago as miraculously as the first Apollo landed on the moon. It ignited the energies of scientists and engineers, industrial tycoons, government and military brass. It stirred the dreams of pioneers, explorers, writers, poets, and composers.

A model railroad is your passport into all of these professions and countless other fields of endeavor. The only limit is your imagination. Whatever restrictions you now place on your own aptitude for science, crafts, or the arts, I guarantee you that as you progress in your model-railroad making, you will be tapping and releasing hidden talents in yourself—and in your family and friends, as well. I know, because that's what happened to me.

Your first step into this wonder-filled world can be as slow and easy as you like. But soon even a little motorless push-pull train or a simple circle of track with a single train running around a table will evoke the sights, sounds, and drama of its prototype—the thunder of the mighty "iron horse," the lonesome shriek of the whistles, the rolling rhythm of wheels along the tracks. At this point, you'll be proceeding ahead at high speed, or *highballing,* toward the building of your model railroad empire. You even have a choice of eras—past, present, or future—for your replica.

The making of miniatures and models reaches back thousands of years, possibly predating the pyramids of ancient Egypt. Today modelmaking is a massive, worldwide industry, providing child and adult hobbyists with the fun and intrigue of working with scaled-down facsimiles of life-size prototypes, and providing big business and the armed forces with instructional and display devices. During World War II, meticulously detailed models were used extensively for tactical planning and to accomplish vital coordination in joint allied operations (one extremely elaborate training aid was a large, room-sized model of a port, complete with every building of the town, every ship in the harbor, and all the shore installations). This was a windfall for amateur modelers.

With the development of plastics, which are extremely flexible and may be machined, stamped, cast, or extruded to any shape, factory production of models burgeoned to include an almost infinite variety of items—at costs more agreeable to the average hobbyist's pocketbook. Most flexible of all are the costs entailed in building a model railroad. A simple *pike* (railroad) that you can be proud of can be assembled for as little as $15, or you can spend as much as your budget will permit. You can acquire your railroad empire gradually, starting simply and adding items as money becomes available. Meanwhile, you'll be running your railroad from the very first day.

Railroading is a hobby that can be enjoyed by all: boys and girls, men and women. There are no age barriers. There are simple, ready-made pikes for youngsters, and complicated ones to be constructed from scratch for adults and more sophisticated buffs.

In this little world your experiences will be truly tremendous. Even your innovations that don't measure up to your original expectations will be enlightening. Even your "disasters"—derailments, collisions, landslides—will be rewarding. When I was a child, every disaster added to my belief in the magical forces at work in my miniature railroad, while raising my dad's blood pressure a notch or two. As an adult, I found that my patience with any experiment that did not meet with instant success became as short-circuited as my father's had been, until a most unusual hazard hit my railroad room.

A Burmese-Manx hybrid kitten, with all the curiosity of its species plus all the expertise of its sire's breed in opening doors, at first was content to sit slit-eyed and silently enthralled on a stretch of "grass." Came the day when it decided to periodically and selectively become actively involved with my operation—sometimes derailing my fast express to Buffalo or sabotaging a stretch of track; once kidnapping a "passenger" waiting on a platform for the 3:05 local; regularly "uprooting" a tree or raiding a pasture to carry off some "livestock." By some strange alchemy of the spirit that all creatures great and small exert on each other, this Godzilla of my pike helped me to see my model railroad empire once again with all my childhood enchantment—and enabled me to write this book with all the needs of a beginner clearly in mind.

VOCABULARY
FOR MODEL RAILROADERS

ALTERNATING CURRENT (AC): Electric current from the household wall socket. (From the power pack, it operates an O gauge railroad, or the accessories of an HO or N gauge pike.)

ARTICULATED: Long steam engine with swiveling wheel trucks.

BALLAST: Crushed stone used for the base of the tracks of prototype railroads.

BLOCK: Track section with one insulated rail, used to stop a loco.

BOILER: Cylindrical tank of a steam engine in which water is heated to steam to power the loco.

BOXCAR: Freight car shaped like an elongated box used usually to transport packaged products.

BRASS HAT: High official of a railroad.

CABOOSE: Last car on a line of freights, used as living quarters for the crew.

CATTLE CAR: Freight car with horizontal slats for sides to allow air circulation for its cargo of cattle or other livestock.

CIRCUIT: Complete route the electric current travels from the power pack through the tracks or accessories back to the power pack.

CIRCUIT BREAKER: Device included in a good power pack that disconnects the electric current automatically when a short circuit occurs. (*See also* SHORT CIRCUIT.)

COG ENGINE: Rare type of steam engine once used for climbing very steep grades.

CORNFIELD COLLISION: Head-on collision usually occurring when tracks ran through a field of high corn, limiting visibility.

COUPLER: Automatic "grab" device that hooks two cars together.

COWCATCHER: Plowlike projection on the front of a steam loco that cleared the rails of minor obstructions (even cows).

CROSSING: Section of track where one train on one track can cross another track at the same level.

CROSSOVER: Elevated track that crosses above another track or surface obstruction.

CURRENT: Flow of electricity along a wire or other conductor.

CYLINDERS: Chambers on the sides of a steam engine into which steam is fed to move pistons and their connecting rods to turn the engine's driving wheels.

DEAD TRACK SECTION: Non-electrified section of track.

DIRECT CURRENT (DC): Electric current which flows in only one direction. (Operates HO and N locos from the power pack.)

DRIVING WHEEL (DRIVERS): Loco wheels turned by the motor.

DUMMY: Diesel engine hooked up behind another diesel engine (called "dummy" because it contains no engineer).

ENGINE: Moving power of a train; either steam or diesel.

FLANGE: Projection on the inside rim of the car or loco wheel that keeps it on the rail.

FLATCAR: Freight car with no sides, sometimes no ends, used for carrying logs, lumber, large machinery, pipe, etc.

FLEX-TRACK: Flexible track in yard lengths easily bent into the desired curvature.

FREIGHT: Freight car or freight train.

FROG: Part in the exact center of the turnout that facilitates passage of train wheels through the turnout. (*See also* TURNOUT.)

FUDGING: Trying to stretch track that's too short (resulting in eventual derailment or broken circuit).

GAPPING: Technical term for separating track sections by insulated rail joiners.

GAUGE: Size of railroad tracks, usually given as the width between rails. Now applied to the scale of model railroads—O gauge=$\frac{1}{48}$ of the prototype; HO=$\frac{1}{87}$ of the prototype; N gauge=$\frac{1}{160}$ of prototype size.

GRAB IRON: Railing along the side of a freight or loco that crewmen hold onto while inspecting or making repairs.

HIGHBALL: Large ball hanging high outside a trackside facility used to signal to the steam loco engineer that he has a clear track ahead and can proceed at speed.

HOG (PIG): Vernacular for a large steam loco.

HO GAUGE: (*see* GAUGE).

HOPPER: Freight car, usually metal with an open top, used to carry loads of coal, ore, and similar material.

HUMPING: Uncoupling a freight car in a yard and allowing it to roll by its own momentum to the desired location, slowed sufficiently by a slight rise in the track called a "hump."

JOINERS: Small shoe-like clips, metal or plastic, used to connect rails in HO and N gauge. Also called RAIL JOINERS.

KIT: Package of parts of a freight, or loco, or structure which you assemble yourself.

KITBASHING: Assembling parts from two or more kits to form a composite structure (a building, car, or even loco).

LIVE RAIL: The rail carrying the outgoing (minus) current from the power pack.

MOW: Cars of a freight train which do not contribute to railroad revenue (service cars, cranes, caboose, etc.).

N GAUGE: (*see* GAUGE).

O GAUGE: (*see* GAUGE).

PIKE: Any railroad line, with tracks and equipment. Can include buildings, terrain, and landscaping.

PILOT (PILOT TRUCK): Leading small wheels of a long loco that direct the front of the loco along the track.

POWER PACK: Electric control unit which converts the 110-volt AC current of the wall outlet to a reduced voltage DC current for the HO or N train and a reduced AC voltage current for the accessories.

PROTOTYPE: Original, life-size unit from which a scaled-down model railroad unit was copied.

RECTIFIER: Part of the power pack that converts the AC current to DC.

REEFER: Refrigerator freight car.

RERAILER: Section of track which facilitates placing wheels of small cars on the rails.

REVERSE LOOP: Track layout containing a loop that returns a train to the main track heading back in the direction from which it came.

ROADBED: Raised level base on which the tracks are laid.

ROLLING STOCK: Freight cars. On some lines passenger cars are also included.

ROUNDHOUSE: A locomotive enginehouse named roundhouse because of its circular shape that was designed to fit the exterior circular turntable that feeds the locomotives into its engine stalls.

SCRATCH BUILDING: Constructing a car, loco, or building from materials not precut or preformed, as they are in a kit.

SET: Preselected tracks and trains ready for quick assembly into a working unit.

SHOE: Electrical conductor that runs on the live rail as the train moves, picking up current, usually for the loco.

SHORT CIRCUIT: Accidental connection between two parts of an electrical circuit that permits the current to return to the power source without performing its work, such as running the loco motor.

SIDING: Track off the main line where a slow train can park to let a faster train have the right-of-way.

SLIP SWITCH: Complicated turnout which allows a train on Track A to switch to Track B, or a train on Track B to switch to Track A.

SPUR: Track leading from a main line to a factory, depot, or rail yard.

STRING: Line of coupled freight cars.

SWITCH: Electrical device for turning current on and off to operate a turnout, lights, or other accessories.

SWITCHER: Small loco, steam or diesel, used to shuffle cars in a rail yard.

TENDER: Small hopper behind the steam loco that carries the coal for the fire that heats the water in the boiler, converting it to steam to drive the loco.

TERMINAL: (1) The electrical contact to which the conducting wire is fastened. (2) End of a track main line. (3) Large railroad station fed by a number of main line tracks.

TIES: Wooden crosspieces on which the track rails are *spiked,* or fastened.

TINPLATE: Name originally applied to model trains stamped from tin, now applied to toy trains not authentically designed from prototypes.

TRAILING TRUCK: Small wheels under the loco's cab.

TURNOUT: Track section which allows a train to turn off the main line. A right-hand turnout sends the train to the right or straight ahead; a left-hand turnout lets it go to the left or straight ahead.

TURNTABLE: Rotary platform which permits a loco to turn completely around or directs it to a specific stall of an enginehouse.

WYE: A Y-shaped turnout which permits a train to go either right or left but not straight ahead.

YARD: Multiple-track location where cars, rolling stock, and strings are assembled, freights are stored, etc.

SECTION I

THE WORLD
OF MODEL TRAINS

The *Skip*, rare model of a push-pull floor train made in 1868. Rather delicate for youngsters, it probably found greater favor among adults. It can be seen in the A & D Toy-Train Village and Railway Museum in South Carver, Massachusetts. (A & D collection)

1. BIRTH OF
THE TRAIN HOBBY

IN THE 1800s A NEW FORM OF TRANSPORTATION—the railroad—revolutionized not only passenger travel and commerce, it also transformed a vast expanse of wilderness sparsely dotted with settlements and Indian villages into one nation—bountiful, unique, and indivisible. When the railroad started carrying carloads of Easterners and immigrants newly-arrived in America out to the virgin territory, the Westward Ho! migration swelled to flood proportions. Where railroad depots were erected, miracles occurred: one-horse outposts became booming towns—for example, Abilene, Kansas, just a little village through the 1850s, burgeoned into a thriving city when Joseph McCoy of Chicago established a depot there and enticed Texan cattlemen to drive their longhorn steers up to Abilene with the then-stupendous offer of $40-a-head. But throughout the Civil War, railroad expansion virtually came to a standstill. Most of the Midwest was practically devoid of railroads; depots were few and far between —after long drives, the steers arrived at their destination as scrawny skeletons of their former selves; farmers' produce spoiled on the journey. With the war's end, the big business tycoons set to turning the dream of a complete transcontinental railroad into a reality.

From the west the Central Pacific steamed eastward over the snow-capped Sierras. From the east the Union Pacific came chugging westward across the Rockies. On May 10, 1869, in the flatlands of Utah that lay in between, the meeting of the two lines was commemorated in the historic, flag-raising Golden Spike ceremony. By the dawn of the twentieth century, a network of major railroads and feeder lines crisscrossed the country, reaching into almost every village and town.

The sight of a locomotive pulling its passenger or freight cars as it thundered through the countryside like some prehistoric, steam-breathing dragon was an awe-inspiring spectacle, especially to youngsters. Since railroads occupied such a prominent place in the American scene, entrepreneurs soon realized there would be a market for toy trains.

The first of these were actually no more than painted blocks of wood, each with four wheels, bearing only a remote resemblance to railroad cars. These blocks were fastened together behind a locomotive to resemble a string of cars, and the assembly was pushed or pulled across the floor. There was no track, and the wheels had no flanges. These "floor trains" are still popular among the kindergarten set, although now they are made of space-age colored plastic as well as wood.

Early in the 1900s the cars and loco were stamped out of metal and a motor was added to the loco. The first such motor was a friction drive. A heavy flywheel was installed in the loco, and pushing the loco several times across the floor caused the flywheel to spin; when released, the loco would travel several feet without being pushed, driven by the momentum of the spinning flywheel. Next an enterprising watchmaker installed a clock spring in a loco and introduced the wind-up clockwork motor. Then the hobbyist, with the addition of flanged wheels on his cars and a circle of track, which had to be custom made because as yet there were no track-size standards, could sit back and watch the train follow the circle all by itself.

As early as 1840 a clever Vermont hobbyist fitted a small electric motor inside a loco and amazed his friends with his train's performance, but his ideas at that time were considered too extreme to be taken seriously. The early metal trains were called "tinplates" because many were stamped from tin. Much of this tin was scrap discarded by makers of such items as cans; in fact, many of these cars still carried the original labels, such as "soup," "syrup," or "beans."

Strange as it may seem, the most ardent modelers of the early days of the train era were inventors, engineers, and locomotive salesmen. Traveling salesmen carry sample cases when they peddle their wares, but a locomotive salesman couldn't tuck a giant steam engine under his arm. He needed a model, perfectly detailed and capable of operating. The company engineer supplied him with one.

One of the first cast-iron floor trains of 1880 made by Wilkins. (A & D collection)

A Joy-Line key wind-up train. Note station by Ives, the prefab tunnel, and early figures. (A & D collection)

It was made of brass, a perfect replica of the real one. It had a tiny boiler, and the water was heated to steam usually by a small alcohol lamp. Many of these fine models, placed in display cases, were later used to decorate the offices of the company presidents.

Inventors, too, had to have finely detailed working models to submit with their plans to the U. S. Patent Office in order to patent their inventions. Many of these have since found their way into the Smithsonian Institution. If you should happen to find one of the above-mentioned brass models, guard it carefully; today it is worth a small fortune to collectors. Working steam locomotives, called "live steamers," were once popular among hobbyists and still are among a few, but they have been largely superseded by the more versatile electric types.

Three steamers, called *live steamers* because they were run by real steam produced by heating the water in the boiler with an alcohol flame. At left is the *Piddler* from the late 1900s; at right is the German version; in the center is the *Dribbler,* a later model from England. (A & D collection)

Until 1900 model railroading was handicapped by the fact that manufacturers had not agreed on a standard track width or train size. Every one had his own preference and once a hobbyist started with a particular manufacturer's offering, he had to stay with that brand or switch exclusively to another. Trains were not interchangeable. But a remedy was attempted in 1900. A British manufacturer publicized what he called No. 1 gauge—about 1¾ inches between the rails— and invited others to follow suit. But another company decided on a slightly larger width and called it No. 2. Then followed still other makers with Nos. 3 and 4.

It is difficult now for us to imagine the toy train world of the early 1900s. The market was literally swamped with toy trains, all different brands in varying sizes. Few makers had adopted the No. 1 gauge. In 1910 the Ives Company, which in 1884 had marketed an electric train, proposed the revolutionary O gauge which was still smaller than the No. 1 gauge. The matter of gauge size has always been important because the larger the train, the more space is required for an interesting track layout. Also, large trains have always been more expensive. The O gauge, with a distance between the rails of only 1¼ inches, was an almost instant success, and today trains of this size, produced almost exclusively by Lionel, still have an appeal for many modelers. The O gauge's main argument for survival, advanced by the manufacturer, is "It is easier for young hands to handle." This is true when it is compared to the currently more popular small gauges.

A gauge still smaller than O was on the horizon. At the Chicago

The oldest train in the A & D Museum, made in 1862 by James C. Fallow Co., Pennsylvania. (A & D collection)

World's Fair of 1933–34 visitors were fascinated by tiny electric loco-motives, each pulling a string of tiny cars around on equally tiny tracks. The distance between the rails was only ⅝ of an inch. It was the brainchild of two Englishmen who called it the HO gauge (Half O). A loco was as small as 4 inches in length. Toy train buffs were ecstatic. A track layout that required a 12-foot table in O gauge, in HO needed only a 6-foot table, and was far less expensive.

World War II caused a lull in model train production, but after the war, production picked up again at an even faster pace. And the ac-ceptance of the HO gauge inspired the introduction of several addi-tional gauges that were even smaller than HO—the TT (table top) gauge and the popular American Flyer trains were absorbed by A. C. Gilbert Company, and then A. C. Gilbert brought out the S gauge, smaller than the O but larger than HO. The HO, however, has been the one that has caught the fancy of model railroaders and now ac-counts for almost 80 per cent of all sales.

The N has grown in popularity because of its size, about half the HO, or about $\frac{1}{160}$ of the prototype. It requires so little space, one modeler built an entire working layout in a violin case. N has acces-sories similar to those of HO although of course in a smaller size, and its operation is similar. A disadvantage of its very small size is that it must be handled carefully. Should you accidentally drop one of the finely detailed N locos, it probably would be damaged irreparably. In HO gauge it might need only minor repair; in O gauge, most of the damage would be to the floor.

The O gauge has another advantage I don't think Lionel mentions: its tracks are so sturdy that a child can step on one without smashing it. I don't advise anyone's attempting this with an HO or N gauge track, however. But the O gauge track leaves much to be desired as far as realistic appearance is concerned. It has three metal ties, one across each end and one across the center. In addition it has a third rail down the center.

One of the factors which inhibited the acceptance of all model trains in their early years was the seeming inability of manufacturers to make the trains authentic replicas of the prototypes. Since World War II, however, trains have been produced for market in reasonably accurate scale. For example: a modern HO loco or car not only resembles its prototype in appearance but is $\frac{1}{87}$ of its size. This actually means that it would take 87 models of an HO loco, placed in line, to equal the length of the large prototype from which it was copied.

2. MODEL RAILROADS TODAY

BEFORE YOU START IN THE MODEL RAILROAD HOBBY, it will be wise to look at it as a whole with all of its ramifications to see what lies before you. The best way to do this is to visit a local model railroad club and watch its trains in operation. Even better would be to attend one of the annual conventions of the NMRA (National Model Railroad Association), where members from all over the country display their finest.

An early Lionel train, similar to the one the author, when a youngster, saw circling the base of the tree when he awoke one Christmas morning.

But the beginner must be prepared for his introduction to a large layout; otherwise the scene may be quite bewildering—several trains running on the same tracks, lights flashing, remote control *turnouts* (switches) snapping open and closed. Maybe several club members will be running the road. It will appear quite complicated and beyond the comprehension of a newcomer. It also will look discouragingly expensive.

Modelers make their layouts (*pikes*) as lifelike as possible with na-
tural-looking tunnels, bridges, highway crossings, factory buildings
with sidings for freights, signal lights, highway traffic (although stationary), passengers and train workers, lakes and rivers, ocean docks,
lumber mills, coal mines, mountains, etc. All of these, except perhaps
the mountains and water features, must be to the HO ($\frac{1}{87}$) scale.

Types of engines and cars vary according to the locality, original
railroad, and time era the modeler wishes to duplicate. Manufacturers
can supply much of this material, even tiny trees if the modeler wants
to cover his mountain with a forest. The modeler usually chooses a
name for his pike, and if he runs a passenger train, he issues tickets to
visitors who wish to see it in operation.

The pikes of some model railroad clubs are so large and complex
that they can't be run by a single engineer; several are needed—an
engineer for each train as well as a central dispatcher. They all have
their responsibilities and take their jobs seriously. They wear regulation trainmen's hats with the name of the club railroad on the front.
In some clubs they talk to each other not by shouting but by means of
a telephone system, using earphones and chest mikes. Trains operate
on a scaled-down time schedule. In the event of an accident such as a
derailment, the dispatcher sends out a loco with a wrecking car and
derrick. Human hands replace the train on the track, but every operation is kept as lifelike as possible.

The newcomer must realize that a large club railroad is not the
product of one person but of all the club members. And they devoted
many hours to assembling it. The costs were shared, too. But even so,
the total expenditure was not necessarily large enough to deplete any
one member's wallet appreciably.

A newcomer, with limited funds to spend, can start small and add
to his pike as circumstances permit. It's almost like financing his
hobby on time, purchasing a new feature for his working railroad
each month. And individual pieces aren't expensive. Of course they
can be if really fine items are desired. After two years, I found I had
spent over $1,000 on my pike. If anyone had told me when I began
that the hobby would have cost me that much, I might have gone in
for matchbook collecting instead. As it was, I hadn't noticed the expenditure, and my pike had been working since the first day. A visit
to your local hobby shop will convince you how really inexpensive the
hobby can be. A $5.00 diesel loco will pull your cars until you accu-

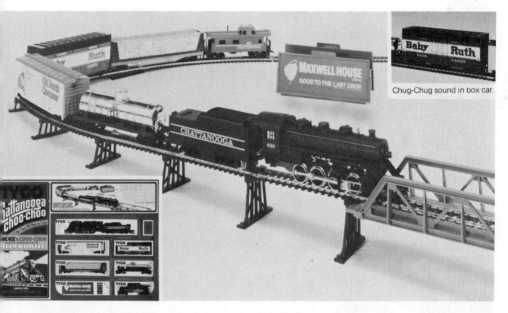

Chug-Chug sound in box car.

The modern Tyco *Chattanooga Choo-Choo* shows how far the model train has developed since its early beginnings during the last century.

mulate enough money for that slick $30 Casey Jones steam loco that has caught your eye.

It should be noted in passing that frequently a youngster's parents will enjoy and have just as much fun with the layout as the boy or girl who put it together. The cartoon that shows a man playing with a set of trains while his young son tugs at his sleeve and asks, "When can I play with it, Dad?" is more fact than fiction.

You don't have to be a genius to be a successful model railroader. There is plenty of literature that will tell you exactly how to assemble, position, operate, and build all the various components, and you will find the various processes relatively simple if you follow instructions carefully.

Many parents are reluctant to start a son or daughter on the model railroad hobby because it involves the use of electricity and so must be dangerous, the hazards being shock and electrical fire. It is true that the railroad operates from the 110-volt wall outlet, but this current is fed to a transformer that reduces the voltage considerably, and the only live conductors the operator might touch are not capable of

A modern passenger station with upper and lower levels. Pikes can
become quite complex.

causing perceptible shock except under extraordinary circumstances.
Because of the low voltage of the electricity fed to the model railroad,
the possibility of its causing a fire is extremely small.

One of the advantages of this hobby is that it can be as simple or as
complicated as you want it. As you go along, if you find you are going
beyond your depth and that your capabilities don't quite measure up
to the job, you can back off and concentrate on refining what you already have. Maybe you visualize a large control panel with a visual
display that tells you whether each of a dozen remote-control turnouts
is open or closed. Nice to have, but it's a wiring job that's a bit too
difficult for most beginners. Best settle for just a few turnouts and
eliminate the light display.

In general the model railroad may seem very complicated to operate at first but it usually isn't. It doesn't work by magic. You'll learn
that part of the secret is the small control panel, which you can build
yourself. To it you connect the wires from the remote-control
switches, and from other electric accessories you may choose to have,

such as houses and buildings that light up when "night" falls, a working drawbridge, a roundhouse for your engines, etc. Only a very elementary knowledge of electricity is necessary to wire such a panel. Running more than one train on a track is also simple. By manipulating electrical switches on your panel you can be sure there's at least one *dead* (nonelectrified) section of track between your trains so they won't collide.

Do not be afraid of a *cornfield* (head-on) collision between two trains; this is almost impossible to accomplish with standard engines, even if you try. Making a steam loco puff smoke is usually a simple trick. Many are designed with this feature; all you have to do is place a drop of smoke liquid down the stack, and as the loco runs, it will puff away. The headlight will automatically light, too, in most models. Getting the loco to emit a *whooo-hoooo* whistle is more difficult, since it requires a special unit usually installed in the engine's tender, but there is an easy solution to this problem, too. Tyco Industries offers a roadside billboard sign that includes a tiny sound mechanism; when the train approaches the sign you can press a button on your control panel and get your *whooo-hoooo,* which will seem to be coming from the engine.

Your train power pack near the panel will regulate the electric current being fed to your engine and thus will regulate its speed—and back it up. The latest such controls enable you to govern engine speed quite realistically. The first electric trains made unreal jackrabbit starts and would stop on a dime. Now trains can start very slowly like their giant cousins, and can creep into a station before stopping completely.

The Lilliputian buildings and scenery of a club pike also impress the newcomer. It seems that fantastic artistic skill was needed to fashion them. Or else they were created by magic. It is true that some of the miniatures may have been designed and laboriously constructed by exceptionally talented modelers, but in the majority of instances the magic has been supplied by a number of skilled manufacturers who can supply prefabricated pieces which you quickly assemble and glue together. And it requires no talent to apply a few drops of glue in the appropriate places.

But the new plastic buildings are shiny, and where in the world do you see a shiny plastic building? The modeler has a remedy for this, too. A quick sweep of a special paint applied from a spray can will give a realistic weather-beaten appearance to the shiny, colored plastic. Buildings or parts of buildings that have been exposed often to the soot from passing locomotives and should therefore be darkened to look real can be made to appear so by the application of a similar spray of a dark, sootlike paint.

Wooden buildings are also available in precut pieces. When assembled and glued, they are colored with special railroad modelers' paint applied with a brush.

A small but elaborate pike assembled from Bachmann products.

Mountains are easily made of covered frameworks and a substance such as plaster of Paris, then painted. Lawns are a liquid paste on which a green material called "phlox" is sprayed to simulate grass. The important thing the modeler must remember is that scenery must be to scale (about $\frac{1}{87}$ of the real thing in HO). In the case of large railroads, the foundation of the tracks and their crossties, called *ballast,* is usually gravel. Of course such gravel on your model pike would be too large; a liquid paste is applied and then tiny sandlike particles are added in the desired color, light tan or gray. This ballast is available at your hobby store. Advanced modelers sometimes lay their own tracks instead of employing the ready-made variety. This is a tedious process; each tie must be carefully set in place and the rail fastened to it with tiny spikes. A continual check must be made during assembly to insure that the rails are the required distance apart.

As you may have realized by now, your greatest expenditure in the model railroad hobby will be time, but you will find it will be well worth it. And remember, as a dedicated modeler you'll be part of a great fellowship. By estimate, the world of model railroads is about as large as the world of tennis, if not in actual size, at least in the number of participants. It is estimated at over a quarter million.

SECTION II

YOUR
FIRST TRAIN

The Atchison, Topeka and Santa Fe, a set by Tyco, contains a steam loco and tender, pulpwood car, cattle car, caboose, cattle depot with cows, fourteen sections of track including a terminal rerailer, and a power pack.

3. ADVANTAGES
OF THE TRAIN SET

THERE'S AN EASY WAY TO START YOUR HOBBY and almost immediately become a railroad engineer although your pike might be only a simple circle; this humble beginning will inspire you to greater things; it is to purchase a ready-to-run (R-T-R) train set. All you have to do is put the tracks together, put the train on them, hook up the power pack, and you're off and running.

An R-T-R set comes in a cardboard box with contents and description printed on the cover. It consists of a locomotive (steam or diesel); cars (passenger or freight); sections of track, two wires, a power pack, and also an instruction booklet. Some sets come without the power pack; if the set you like has no power pack, you can purchase one separately.

In most sets, all the track sections are curves and there will be enough to make a circle. Some sets have a few straight sections, too, so you can make an oval instead of a circle. One section probably will be a *rerailer,* with center and sides raised so they are flush with the tops of the rails. This is to facilitate placing the cars on the track properly—not as simple as it may seem, especially for N gauge cars with their tiny wheels. One track section may be a *terminal* track with two terminals which you connect to the plainly marked terminals of the power pack with wires. Plug the power pack cord into the 110-volt wall outlet and, with your track sections connected, you're ready to roll your train. Your power pack has a throttle; turn it one way and the loco will move forward. Turn it the other way and the loco will stop. Some power packs also have a reverse switch; flip it and the current will reverse and the loco will back up.

Before you buy your set you must decide which size railroad you prefer—O, HO, or N. These are the three sizes we'll discuss. Other gauges are generally too offbeat to be considered by a beginner.

The O gauge is fine if you want your train to be primarily a toy. Realistic accessories are limited, but you can lay your tracks on the floor and disassemble them and put them away in their box when you've finished playing with them. When I was a youngster, my first train was an O gauge. I awoke one Christmas morning to find it running around the Christmas tree. Long after I outgrew it, every Christmas it ran around the new tree. It finally became a memento of my age of innocence.

The HO or N are preferred if you take your railroad hobby seriously and intend to expand it eventually, adding scenery and a multitude of accessories. For a beginner, HO will prove to be simpler than the N because it is larger. But don't run either one on the floor; the small engine will pick up dust and lint and give you trouble.

You should plan to mount the tracks permanently on a solid surface such as a large table. The elevated table surface will also enable an adult to operate your train without stooping over and cricking his back. I have found a Ping-Pong table satisfactory for an HO pike. Lay on its surface a 4 by 6 foot sheet of fiber material such as half-inch-thick Homosote. Many modelers use plywood because it is more durable; but Homosote is less expensive, easy to cut, and nails go into it very easily.

There is also the fact that a train running on plywood can rattle loudly enough to fray everybody's nerves, while the fiber Homosote deadens sound. The tracks and accessories can be nailed to it with little difficulty. HO tracks should always be nailed in place, otherwise vibration and the pressure of a train rounding a curve will gradually weaken the train connections. Nails of the correct size are available at your hobby shop.

The above advice for HO also applies to N trains. A simple N pike may take little room on a 4 by 6 foot surface, but think of all the room you have for expansion! Or you can cut the Homosote to 3 by 4 or smaller if you desire. And then, if your pike has no loose scenery or accessories, you can slide it under a bed or stand it up behind a door when you want it out of the way. At first you might favor this arrangement, but soon you will reach the stage of a connoisseur when

This Tyco kit contains everything needed to expand a simple oval track into a layout 4 by 8 feet. Instructions are included for wiring track and for operating two trains.

pride and admiration of your handiwork will prevent your putting it out of sight even temporarily.

What is the cost of train sets? Not as high as you might imagine. At the date of this writing, during the peak of inflation, there still are bargains. Generally the most inexpensive train sets are those with diesel locos rather than steam locos. Sets offered by Bachmann Brothers are among the finest. Among their offerings is the HO gauge *The Bullet*. It has an *EMD F-9* diesel with headlight, a flatcar with logs, a *hopper* (the type of car that carries coal or similar ores), a *reefer* (refrigerator car), a *caboose,* a "blinking" bridge and trestle set with a blinking warning light, and enough track to make a 36 by 45 inch oval. A power pack and instructions are included. The list price is about $39.50. More expensive is Bachmann's *Rail Blazer,* with enough track to make two ovals measuring 45 by 45 inches and an oil tank which emits the diesel's whistle. Tyco Industries makes a

The *Bullet*, a train set by Bachmann, contains a diesel engine with headlight, a log car with logs, a refrigerator car, a hopper, a caboose, an eighteen-piece bridge and trestle set with blinking light, track, power pack, and instructions.

number of less expensive starter kits. They also offer the Layout Expander system with which you can expand a simple oval track into a larger two-train layout. Backmann also makes a number of excellent N gauge sets.

I must emphasize that any prices given in these pages are list prices. These are often discounted by large mail-order retailers, such as America's Hobby Center in New York, which publishes a periodic bulletin listing over one thousand discount items. If you have to buy a separate power pack, the Model Rectifier Corporation (MRC) manufactures a good one for as little as $15.

Before purchasing a set, you might give some thought to what you want your railroad eventually to be. If you favor a romantic era of the steam engine, you'll find that the diesel, no matter how beautiful, will have no place in the steam-age layout you will perfect some day; and so you had better pass up the diesel for a steamer set.

Before buying any train set, open the box in front of the salesman and carefully check the contents. The pieces included are usually listed on the box cover or on an enclosed parts list. Be sure the instruction booklet hasn't been removed.

Inspect the cars and engine for signs of wear or damage. You want to be sure it isn't a set that has been returned for faulty operation, then inadvertently been replaced on the sales shelf.

Sets sometimes contain imperfections not visible by inspection, such as a loco headlight that is supposed to light but doesn't. Most of these are minor and if any become evident when you try the set at home, return the set and the salesman will remedy it quickly or replace it. Some stores have a stretch of track where the loco can be tested immediately. To replace defective items in a mail-order set, return the entire set, insured, to the seller with a letter of explanation.

Of course, it is too much to expect a budding new model railroad engineer who has just bought a fascinating new train set to take it home and then stifle his or her enthusiasm by stuffing the set in a closet until a sheet of Homosote and a discarded Ping-Pong table can be obtained upon which to assemble it. The normal impulse to assemble the set and start the trains running as soon as possible needn't be repressed.

Again I caution you not to run the HO or N gauge trains on a rug, no matter how close or worn the nap of the rug may be, because of the susceptibility of the small motors to lint and dust.

Almost any table will serve as a temporary surface even if you can't nail down the tracks. If two sections loosen and come apart after a couple of runs, as they surely will, just reconnect them. A card table is large enough for an N-gauge circle—perhaps even an HO circle, but it will be close. A cleared kitchen table is often used, also.

But don't use a polished surface such as a dining room table before first protecting it with a thin tablecloth or a folded bed sheet. The plastic ties of the tracks can scratch a polished tabletop. Moreover, on any slippery surface, your simple layout will skid all over the place. I remember years ago I put together an HO kit on a polished table. The momentum of the train, plus its vibration, moved it across the table, and only gymnastic action on my part kept my dream pike from plunging to the floor. Even a card table is too slippery to be trusted without a covering. On an adequately large surface, you can expand your initial circle by adding a few straight sections of track, which must be purchased separately.

If a second train set catches your eye, and you feel compelled to purchase it also, you can run both train sets separately or combine the tracks into one layout. The store clerk will show you how, or study chapters 7 and 11.

For a second set, however, a wiser choice might be one in the other gauge: N if you already have an HO, or HO if your first set is an N. After trying out both, you can decide with which gauge you wish to build your future empire. Whichever gauge you favor, the other set will not be a total loss; you'll find a use for it eventually.

It's best to decide which gauge you prefer by testing both, before you invest in additional locos and cars, buildings and accessories.

4. THE STORY
OF LOCOMOTIVES

IF YOU DECIDE TO BUY YOUR RAILROAD piece by piece, your first selection will probably be the locomotive. And if you want your pike to be as authentic as possible, you'll want to choose the right one to do the job you want it to do—pull passenger cars, or long or short strings of freights, or work in a rail yard. For this you must first be familiar with the various types of locos. They are designated by the same names, numbers, and symbols as their prototypes.

In general there are three types of steam locos: *switchers* for shuttling cars and making up trains in a rail yard, light engines for short strings of freight and level ground, and heavy engines for long strings of freights and mountainous country. There are also fast, light, and heavy engines for pulling passenger cars. Actually the power of the engine will seldom be a problem on your model railroad. If your engine has too heavy a load to pull or a grade too steep to climb, in most cases the wheels will turn but the loco will be too light to give them traction, and they will skid on the rails.

Actually your model switcher engine will be capable of pulling long freights or passenger cars around your pike regardless of distance. The same is true of light engines. But on actual railroads every engine type has its own specific function. A switcher was almost never seen on an open track, and the same should be true of your pike if you want authenticity. In Europe an engine called the *cog engine* was popular for pulling cars up very steep slopes. A rotating cog below the engine engaged a serrated center track to provide the extra traction. A few modelers have pikes and models to simulate this type of

Difference in size between HO loco (top) and N loco (bottom).

operation, but it never became popular in this country and is now unavailable.

A primary consideration in selecting a loco is whether it is short enough to negotiate the tightest curve of the track you have planned. Of course, many modelers choose their locos first and then build their track curvature to fit them. Most switchers will take the tightest curves without derailing. A long engine, such as an articulated one, will operate beautifully on a straight track but the curves must be gradual ones.

Steam engines are designated by a number and a symbol, both showing the number of wheels. And by a name, which is the same as that of its prototype. One of the light freight locos is named the *Prairie*. It is number 2-6-2; its symbol is oOOOo. These indicate that it has one pair of small wheels under the front (leading or pilot truck), three pairs of large driving wheels, and one pair of small wheels under the cab (trailing truck). A fast passenger loco is the *Atlantic,* a 4-4-2 or ooOOo—two pairs of small wheels on the leading truck, two pairs of large drivers and one pair of small wheels on the trailing truck.

Following is a list of the most common steam locos you will encounter:

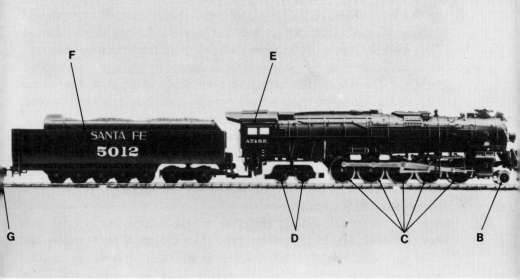

Parts of a loco: A—cowcatcher, B—pilot truck (two wheels), C—drivers (ten wheels), D—trailing (rear) truck (four wheels). This loco is a 2-10-4. Also: E—cab, F—tender, and G—coupler.

Switchers:　4–0 (OO), 0–6–0 (OOO) and 0–8–0 (OOOO)
　　　　(A small switcher such as 0–4–0 without a coal tender
　　　　is usually called a *tank* switcher.)

Freight locos:	Mogul 2–6–0 (oOOO)
	Consolidation 2–8–0 (oOOOO)
	Prairie 2–6–2 (oOOOo)
	Mikado 2–8–2 (oOOOOo)
	Berkshire 2–8–4 (oOOOOoo)
Freight or Passenger:	American 0–4–0 (OO)
	Mountain 4–8–2 (ooOOOOo)
	Northern 4–8–4 (ooOOOOoo)
Passenger locos:	Atlantic 4–4–2 (ooOOo)
	Pacific 4–6–2 (ooOOOo)
	Hudson 4–6–4 (ooOOOoo)
Freight articulated:	2–6–6–2 (oOOO OOOo)
	4–6–6–4 (ooOOO OOOoo)
	2–8–8–2 (oOOOO OOOOo)

The articulated loco wasn't stressed above because it isn't a common type. Very powerful, it saw limited use in real life but as a model it is attractive to some hobbyists. It has three or four pairs of driving wheels set on swiveling trucks beneath the engine so they can turn with the curve of the track and thus help the long loco make the turn.

Note: The size of the leading, or pilot, truck often indicates the use of a steam loco. No small wheels typify a switcher; two small wheels a freight; four small wheels a passenger or fast freight.

Many model steam engines come with "smoke"; this means that their stacks will puff smoke while the locos are moving. The directions with the loco will advise you that to start your loco smoking you must first put a drop or two of "smoke liquid" down the stack; this is converted into the smoke.

Other locos will emit a chugging sound. Many, but not all, will have an operating headlight. In most cases the small bulb causing the light will burn brightly while the loco is stationary but will dim as the loco uses its power to run. The reason is obvious when you think about it; the loco's motor and the headlight receive their electric energy from the track, and when the motor is operating at full power, there isn't much power left for the headlight. A few motors advertise headlights that burn at a constant intensity. A few steam locos also have the *whooo-hoooo* whistle but usually this sound must be added as an accessory.

So when you're shopping for a steam loco, whether it has smoke, headlight, or sound might also influence your selection.

There are also a number of diesel engines popular with modelers. In actual service the cleaner diesel, introduced to railroads about 1934, soon replaced the steam locomotives, even before ecologists began warning about air pollution. The internal combustion diesel engine burns oil rather than coal and does it efficiently, therefore consuming less fuel.

In the diesel-electric loco, the engine drives generators which produce electricity which feeds the motors driving the wheels with unusual smoothness. Diesels have a more complicated system of numbers and letters for identification than steam locos, but if you are primarily interested in duplicating a modern railroad, such as an Amtrak line, you'll soon learn to know them by their appearance characteristics, such as shape of the nose, number of wheels, etc. It's like learning to identify the name and year of a modern automobile from its hood and

Modern version of an old-time 4-4-0 *Jupiter*. Rear pair of drivers is under the cab.

Pennsylvania 2-8-0 *Consolidation.*

The 2-8-2 *Mikado.*

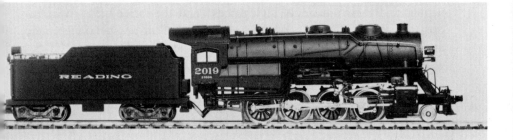

Reading 2-8-0 *Consolidation.*

Amtrak *EMD F-40* diesel.

body shape. The most common diesels you're apt to meet are the *F-3 Streamliner,* the *Alco,* the *GP-9* and the *GP-20.* There are also diesel switchers, such as the *SW-1.* The selection of HO diesels is a large one, and prices are relatively low, in spite of inflation.

The price of a satisfactory R-T-R loco is well within reach of every modeler. Here are prices listed in the 1979 bulletin of America's Hobby Center (AHC) in New York; others you'll find in the advertisements in *Model Railroader* magazine. When you're shopping, don't confuse an R-T-R with a kit, which is usually cheaper but which you must assemble yourself. AHC offers a *Pacific* 2-6-2 steam loco with smoke and a headlight made by the Model Power company for $18.95 (list price $40). The 0-4-0 *Shifter* (a switcher) with headlight and tender is $11.99. A Tyco old-time 4-4-0 and tender is $29.95 (list price $42). A Tyco 2-8-0 *Consolidation* with headlight and tender is $27.95 (list price $36). Diesels run from $10.95 up. All the above locos are HO. The N gauge locos are generally slightly higher in price (except the switchers) because of the difficulty in assembling the smaller parts.

Another series of steam locos will fascinate you by both their beauty and their unusually high prices (and the latter seem to be increasing daily). These locos are finely detailed all-brass models made and assembled in Japan, Taiwan, and other Far Eastern countries where such handiwork is inexpensive. In U.S. stores, their prices range upward from $500. Beware of cheaper models; they usually contain imperfections. They are powered and can run on a pike, but most modelers who can afford them keep them as collectors' items or as investments because their prices are continually rising.

When you purchase a steam loco or a diesel, you will usually be offered a selection of railroad names, such as Rock Island, Santa Fe, or New York Central, each model colored according to the road colors of its prototype. As you progress in your hobby, you'll find that removing the name (with an ink eraser) and replacing it with a name of your own choosing, perhaps one you have invented yourself, will be simple, requiring a sharp eye but little artistic ability.

5. ROLLING STOCK

ROLLING STOCK INCLUDES THE PASSENGER CARS AND FREIGHTS. These produce revenue for the railroad. Also included are the MOWs—the free riders which contribute no revenue, such as the caboose that provides living quarters for the freight's crew, and the maintenance cars for railroad repair. Your selection of passenger cars will depend largely on the time era of your railroad, from the old-fashioned type of the 1800s to the modern *Metroliner* cars. Some are available with lighted interiors. But perhaps you would prefer to add the lights yourself at a later date. Some modelers go all out and even add seats, which can be purchased ready-made, or which you can make yourself.

The largest selection will be that of freight cars, of which there seem to be an endless variety. The most common are boxcars, stockcars for cattle or other animals, reefers, ore cars for coal and other bulk loads, tankers for liquids, flatcars for large cumbersome loads including heavy machinery, logging cars, and automobile carriers. In the passenger category are coaches, sleepers, observation cars, baggage cars, a combination of baggage and passenger, and also the modern double-level vista-dome cars. Maintenance cars include snowplows, cars carrying derricks, cranes, and track or train repair machinery. Rolling stock, too, is offered in a variety of road names.

For younger beginners, the better choice of rolling stock is usually the freights. A youngster becomes tired more quickly of a loco pulling several passenger cars which are all basically alike. But a string of freights, all different, which can be arranged in different orders, pro-

Three types of MOWs. Bottom: crane car and floodlight car. Center: crane and boom cars. Top: floodlight car with adjustable light.

Automobile carrier.

Caboose with mail pickup platform and moving figure.

Freight with cube-type boxcar, three-dome tank car, log flatcar, hopper, and caboose.

vides greater scope for the imagination. The addition of a tunnel also adds interest.

R-T-R freights are priced at approximately $2.00 for the simpler models such as the boxcars, and $3.00 for the more complex tank cars and reefers. Working models, such as a gondola that can dump its load of coal or sand, are proportionately higher in price. The simplest R-T-R passenger cars carry a price tag of about $3.00, more with lights. The most expensive passenger cars seem to be the old-timers, their prototypes dating back to the late 1800s.

No matter which cars you choose, eventually you will become dissatisfied with the newness of their appearance, and you will embark on a new phase of your hobby—weathering, which was mentioned briefly previously and will be discussed more fully in chapter 9. The caboose is a prime target for weathering. Who, except its manufacturer, has ever seen a sparkling, clean caboose that hasn't been "through the mill"? Your first freights will be shiny plastic too, and they will have to be dulled to look authentic.

The cars hook to each other by couplers, as do the prototypes, and the lead car hooks to the tender of the loco by the same means. These tiny couplers work as if by magic. Just roll one car against another and the two will automatically couple. Back a loco against a string of freights or passenger cars; start the loco forward and the string will follow. At first you will uncouple (disconnect) cars with your fingers or use a tiny rod which you can insert between two cars from above, but eventually you will install a magnetic uncoupler on a section of your track.

Bring your cars so the coupler is over the uncoupler track, back up slightly, and the coupler will open, freeing the two cars from each

Bachmann's *Comet*. Passenger cars produce revenue for the railroad and so are not MOWs.

other. You might even want to install a remote-control uncoupler made by Kadee on a certain section of track. Then you can just press a switch on your control panel and the cars over the track will uncouple. Most cars come with plastic couplers installed, but many modelers ignore them, as you will when you get further into the hobby; they install instead a special metal coupler made by Kadee. The automatic uncouplers mentioned above are magnetic, and won't work with plastic couplers.

Don't purchase the first freight car you see. There are many beautiful ones in attractive colors and configurations. Probably, like most novice modelers, you'll be so impressed by the large assortment that on your first trip to the model shop you'll buy a dozen. If your eyes are bigger than your pike, don't fret; you'll find uses for all the freights eventually.

6. DO-IT-YOURSELF KITS

AT THE BEGINNING, the easiest way to get off to a flying start is to use R-T-R, as I described in the previous chapter—simply buy locos, freight cars, and buildings fully assembled for instant operation. But it's less expensive and more rewarding to buy them in kit form and assemble them yourself. In some cases you will have an even greater selection of models by using kits.

Assembling a kit is not as difficult as it may seem. Kits vary from the very simple to the complex. The former may take only a few minutes and require no more than some glue for the buildings and a screwdriver for the rolling stock. Hence the simple car kits are called screwdriver kits.

Athearn, Inc., is one of the leading manufacturers of rolling stock kits. Car parts are of colored plastic and come with a flat weight that must be glued to the inside of the car floor to provide stability. A tiny control wheel is also supplied, if appropriate, to be glued to the car, usually horizontally to one end of the roof, to simulate reality. In most cars the only use of the screwdriver is to fasten the two four-wheeled trucks to the car's base. Sometimes an underframe is included to be glued underneath the base of the car to represent support ribs, brake cylinder, and similar mechanisms.

The tank of a tank car may have caps to be glued in position, hand rails, and other accessories included in the kit. The more experienced you become in assembling kits, the faster you can do it. The final step is gluing the couplers in position, either the plastic ones that come with the kit or Kadee couplers, which are inexpensive but must be

Loco and circus car assembled from one of the first build-it-yourself kits of the late 1800s. (A & D collection)

Easy to assemble is the track-cleaning diesel from Model Die Casting, Inc., sold under the trade name, Roundhouse.

purchased separately. After final assembly, roll the car against another which has already been tested and okayed to check the action of the coupler. It should open against the other coupler, grab its hook, and close, ready to go.

From this simple type you will eventually graduate to more complicated car kits. These will have some wooden parts which will require sanding and fitting as well as gluing. And they usually have better metal wheels and trucks. Further up the scales are wooden kits, more authentically designed with more details. A wooden boxcar, stockcar, or flatbed is more realistic than one of plastic. Of course, the wood will have to be sanded smooth and painted according to the colors you have chosen for your road or those of the road you are copying.

Loco kits can be extremely complicated, so choose simple ones until you've had some assembly experience. Model Die Casting, Inc., issues some simple diesel kits under the brand name of Roundhouse. Later you might try one of their finer, more difficult kits such as their *Consolidation* steam engine. If at first your fingers seem to be all thumbs when you try to position the side rods, just take a rest and try again; handling and assembling miniature parts is largely a skill that must be learned.

Tyco offers rather simple kits of small steam locos. In the future you might want to add details to these—tiny simulated lamps, for example. Steam locos, except the small switchers, come with tenders, which are simpler than the locos to assemble. Simulated lamps can be added to these, too. Even these lamps must be assembled: in HO, each may be the size of the head of a wooden match; to a small concave spot on the side of the lamp you must glue a speck of diamond-shaped colored glass, either green or red. The simulated headlight on a loco is a larger piece of glass shaped like a diamond with its rear coated to increase reflection; this is glued on the headlight frame of the loco. In room light, it can shine realistically.

In addition to a screwdriver, a most necessary tool needed for assembling a loco from a kit is a small file. The metal parts are usually formed by casting, and frequently where the molds meet some of the molten metal creeps out to form what is called a *flashing*. These flashings must be removed with the file. Openings in a casting, such as screw holes, are often blocked by flashings, also. This file work is neither difficult nor time consuming. Flashings should be removed before assembly and painting.

Kits for buildings are among the easiest to assemble and glue together, and the variety of buildings is almost endless—from Tyco, Model Power, Suydam, Kibri, and others. Campbell, too, is a well-known name in building kits. Their kits include shingles, molded plastic windows and doors, and signs; the parts are made of precision-cut wood. Some of the intriguing kit names are Town School House, Susannah's Frocks, Sherry's Scarlet Slipper Saloon, Columbia Gazette Office, Norm's Landing Boat Shop, and Quincy Oil Warehouse and Office.

Campbell also offers kits for trestles, bridges, and stations. There's even one for a beautiful suburban church with stained-glass windows. Some kits with simple names require a considerable amount of skill to assemble, however. Before purchasing one, inform the salesman of

Typical boxcar kit, from Athearn. Assembly takes only a few minutes.

ASSEMBLY INSTRUCTIONS:

STEEL & WOOD 40' BOX CARS

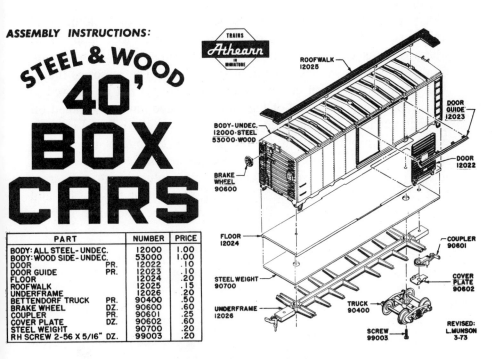

PART		NUMBER	PRICE
BODY: ALL STEEL - UNDEC.		12000	1.00
BODY: WOOD SIDE - UNDEC.		53000	1.00
DOOR	PR.	12022	.10
DOOR GUIDE	PR.	12023	.10
FLOOR		12024	.20
ROOFWALK		12025	.15
UNDERFRAME		12026	.20
BETTENDORF TRUCK	PR.	90400	.50
BRAKE WHEEL	DZ.	90600	.60
COUPLER	PR.	90601	.25
COVER PLATE	DZ.	90602	.60
STEEL WEIGHT		90700	.20
RH SCREW 2-56 X 5/16"	DZ.	99003	.20

ROOFWALK 12025

DOOR GUIDE 12023

BODY- UNDEC. 12000-STEEL 53000-WOOD

BRAKE WHEEL 90600

DOOR 12022

FLOOR 12024

COUPLER 90601

STEEL WEIGHT 90700

COVER PLATE 90602

UNDERFRAME 12026

TRUCK 90400

SCREW 99003

REVISED: L. MUNSON 3-73

Assembly instructions included with each Athearn kit. Parts are listed with prices in case replacements are needed.

the railroad store that you're a newcomer to the hobby and ask him if the kit you desire would be too much of a problem for you.

Some of the building kits in the store will be unsealed. Open the one that interests you and check quickly to be sure it's all there. A loco or car kit will contain a list of parts, with quantities for each. At home, check the contents against this list to be sure the kit is complete. If the box was sealed when you bought it, it probably will be. Any incomplete kit can be returned to the store for replacement. A minor missing part, or a vital part that you have inadvertently damaged, can be replaced; if the store disclaims responsibility, simply write a letter of explanation to the manufacturer and enclose the number of the part.

When gluing plastic parts, be sure to apply the glue sparingly. Some glues will dissolve plastic and the result will be unsightly swellings and warping. When examining a kit with tiny parts, be careful not to lose any of them. Best transfer them to an empty plastic pill bottle. Remember, if any are lost, duplicates can be obtained from the manufacturer.

A popular glue for plastic parts, such as those of buildings and freighters, is Testor's; it is easy to apply. A glue for metal parts? There is an excellent one called ZAP, but it must be used with caution and not by a youngster without supervision. The reason is that it will glue not only metal but also skin, and it should not be allowed to get on the fingers. The end of the applicator tube must be cleaned off immediately after use, but even so it frequently seals shut and must be opened with a pin or needle for the next use. In spite of the precautions necessary in its use, it does an excellent job. Be sure the closed tube is placed where it won't be accidentally confused with a different tube. A friend grabbed his ZAP instead of a similar tube of oil and applied it to a loco's motor. The motor had to be discarded; it froze solid.

7. THE TRACKS

To UNDERSTAND THE FUNCTIONS of model railroad track, you should know the basic principles of electricity. You've noticed that a battery, as well as the DC portion of your power pack, has two terminals, a plus (+) and a minus (−). The electricity, consisting of minute packages of energy called electrons, flows from the minus terminal of the battery when it is connected to the plus terminal by a wire or other conductor. The same is true of the DC terminals of the power pack. This electricity, called the electric current, flows in one direction (from minus to plus) and so is called *direct current* (DC) to distinguish it from *alternating current* (AC), which reverses direction regularly. AC is the current from your wall socket. Of course you must *never* directly connect the two terminals with a wire because the surge of current would be so great it would damage the power source.

But if you allow the electrons to lose some of their energy by doing some work on their way from minus to plus, their return flow to plus will be diminished sufficiently so that they will not damage the power source. Electrons allowed to flow from minus to plus without doing sufficient work cause a condition known as a *short circuit*, which obviously must be avoided. The work done by electrons in your HO railroad is turning the motor of your loco. AC current, in some ways more efficient than DC, lights the bulbs and works most of the accessories in HO gauge, and provides all the power for an O gauge railroad.

Unlike actual railroad tracks, the tracks in your model pike not only constitute the rails on which the trains roll, they also carry the electric current which turns the motor in the loco. For electricity to do work, a circuit is necessary. The electric cord of any appliance looks like a single wire but actually encloses two wires. A single wire run from the wall socket to a lamp will not light the electric bulb; there must be a second wire to carry the electricity back to the wall socket, completing the circuit. In your model railroad, similarly, electric current must be conducted to the motor and another conductor must carry it back to your power pack.

In O gauge, the conductor to the motor is the center rail. The engine picks up the current by the *shoe,* which rides on this *live* rail. After the current passes through the motor, causing it to turn, driving the wheels, it passes through the metal body of the loco to the outside rails, which carry it back to the power pack. With the two-rail HO and N gauges, one rail conducts current to the engine (the live rail), the other rail brings it back. Either rail may be used as the live rail; usually the right-hand rail is chosen (bottom rail on a track running from left to right, top rail on a track running from right to left).

In O gauge, tracks are fastened one to another by a large pin on each rail that fits into a corresponding opening on the rail of the next section of track. In HO gauge, rails of a track section are attached to the next section by rail *joiners,* small metal shoes into which the ends of the rails are inserted. If this arrangement is new to you, the salesman of your railroad store can demonstrate it to you in a second. These rail connections must be tight in order to conduct electricity efficiently. Twisting two connected HO tracks while assembling them or taking them apart can spread the two rail joiners, making them too loose to hold rails tightly enough. They should be tightened carefully with a pair of sharp-nosed pliers, or discarded in favor of new ones; they are very inexpensive.

The tracks supplied with your HO or N train set are classified as sectional because they come in sections. In HO the straight sections are about 9-inches long. Tracks in many sets are supplied by the Atlas Tool Company. Atlas calls them "snap-track," perhaps because they're a snap to assemble. The rails are set on black plastic ties. Challenging their popularity is another brand, Tru-Track, made by Tru-Scale Models, Inc., another busy maker of model supplies. Its advantage is that the plastic ties are grained to simulate wood and are positioned unevenly as they are in an actual railroad, so they look

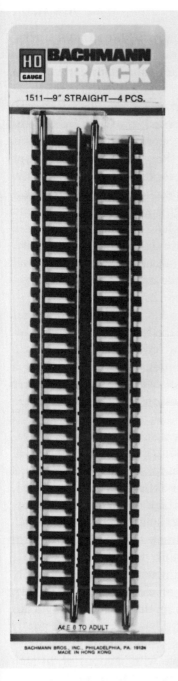

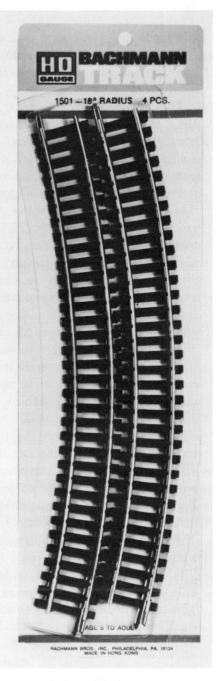

Tracks may be packaged in sets of four, or may be purchased separately. Note that curvature of these HO tracks (right) is designated on the package—in this case, 18 inches.

more authentic. Of course, you will eventually ballast all your tracks, anyhow, in the interest of realism. Tru-Tracks fit together the same way and will connect easily to the snap-track, and both varieties can be used on the same pike.

The advantage of sectional track far outweighs any disadvantages. On a large pike where many sections are used, the large number of track joiners necessary increases the likelihood of loose connections and poor electrical contact. But consider the great advantage—your pike setup can be changed, added to, or rerouted with little difficulty. Another track type, which might be called sectional although the sections are much longer, is ready-track. Lengths are 2 feet or more, and rails are fastened to a strip of finished wooden roadbed stained with a topping of gray ballast. The wooden ties are also stained realistically. Sections are ready to use and can be fastened together with rail joiners. This type is the most realistic in appearance, but as you might expect, it is also more expensive.

If your first track is a simple circle or oval, you'll soon find that your train traveling around and around on the same course grows monotonous. The addition of a station and a few buildings, perhaps a tunnel, will help add interest, but the addition of more track and a couple of *turnouts,* to allow your train to switch tracks, is a surer cure. You can lay out your proposed expansion on paper first, before assembling the necessary additional track.

In planning your track, an important consideration is the curvature, or abruptness of the curves. It is obvious that a long loco will not be able to follow a curve that is too sharp. It will derail, perhaps not every time it tries the curve, but often enough to be a nuisance. Fortunately curved sections of HO and N track come in different curvatures. The most common HO curve is designated "18-inch radius." That is, if enough sections (eight) of this track are assembled to form a circle, that circle will have an 18-inch radius.

Such a curve, 36 inches (3 feet) in diameter, will fit comfortably on a 4-foot square base leaving 6 inches of clearance on each side. This clearance should be considered a minimum since running your track close to the edge of your table isn't advisable: an accidentally derailed train could drop to the floor and would probably be damaged. Of course, broader curves are possible with sections of 24-inch or 30-inch radius. But these require more space, which you might not have available. And there are tighter curves—15 inches, for example. The 18-inch curves are the ones supplied with most sets.

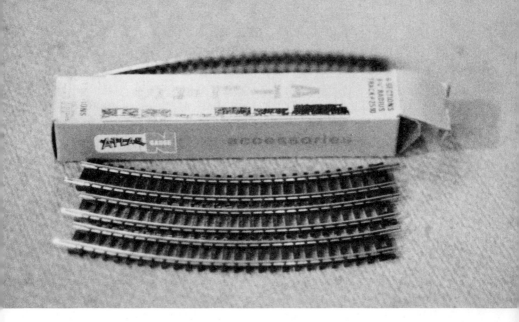

The smaller N gauge tracks often come in boxes of six.

This curvature on an HO train will be satisfactory for almost all diesel and steam locos you might add to your railroad, except the 4-8-4 *Northern,* the 4-6-4 *Hudson,* the 2-8-4 *Berkshire,* and the articulated types, which must have broader curves. But manufacturers' design specifications vary, and a loco of one brand might not take an 18-inch radius while the same loco of another brand will. The best thing to do is ask the hobby shop salesman to test the loco in the store. If he doesn't have an 18-inch radius curve, but is sure it will fit, tell him you will test it on your own track and if it doesn't fit, you'll return it. If he doesn't agree, skip it and look for another loco you can be sure of. The 15-inch curves can be used in your train yard, where the short, slow switch engines will negotiate them with no trouble.

Freight and passenger cars, which have swiveling trucks, will usually take tight turns without derailing. In O gauge the standard curvature is larger (21-inch radius); in N gauge it is smaller (a tiny 9 inches). You can also purchase short sections of track—1-inch long, 1½, 2, 2½, etc. These come in handy when you find a gap in your layout where the two final tracks won't quite meet and the gap isn't large enough to take a full section.

After your tracks are assembled, even if they are only those of your first set, run your hand back and forth over the track connections. They should feel smooth; if one doesn't, but has a sharp projection, check the rail joiner. It probably isn't fitted correctly and will cause a derailment.

Still another type of track, one that often solves annoying problems, is called "flex-track" (flexible track). It comes in 3-foot sections and can be used straight or curved. To curve it, simply grasp the ends and bend it into the desired curvature, tight or broad. When you release it, it will snap straight again; therefore in assembly, nail one end on your layout and continue to nail it down at various points as you bend it into the desired curve. You'll find nail holes in the plastic ties at convenient distances; in regular sectional track and turnouts, the holes appear only in the end ties.

Use small ½-inch nails available at your hobby shop. They are especially easy to drive in place when the foundation of your pike is composition Homosote. The secret of the flexible track is that the rails slide through the tiny projections that hold them to the ties. After you have established your curve, you'll find that one rail will project from the end, being longer than the other because the track has been curved. The excess can be cut off easily with a razor saw, an inexpensive but handy tool you can buy at the railroad shop. You'll find it will have many uses in your hobby. When you make a curve with flex-track, check its radius to make sure it isn't too tight a curve. With a pencil, continue the curve freehand into a full circle and measure its diameter. Regular track sections fit to flex-track with the same rail joiners.

When a life-size train turns from one track onto another, people say it "switches" from one track to the other, and the part of the track which causes this is generally called the switch. But in model railroads it is called a turnout to avoid confusion with the word "switch" as applied to *electrical* switches, which operate lights and other electrical accessories. In fact, the remote-control turnout is operated by an electrical switch.

Turnouts are designated by number. A turnout has a movable section of track. In a right-hand turnout, whether operated by a small hand lever (manual switch) or by remote control, when the movable piece of track is pointed straight ahead, the train rolls along it and continues on the track attached to the front of the turnout.

When the movable track is turned slightly to the right by operation of the lever or by remote control, the train follows it to the right and connects to a short curved piece which is in turn connected to rails that bear off to the right. A left-hand turnout similarly can direct a

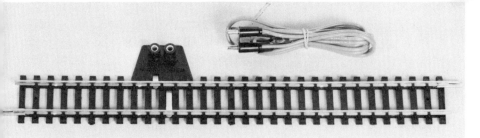

The terminal track has plug-in connectors on the leads. Other ends of leads connect to the power pack.

The curved turnout. Note both main line and side turn to the left. This turnout permits a turn from a curved section of track.

train to the left. In short, a turnout can permit a train to continue straight ahead or can turn it onto a new set of tracks heading in a side direction. This new direction begins as a turn. It can continue as a turn or as a straight stretch of track, depending on which track section you add to that end of the turnout.

The degree of side curvature of a turnout is designated by number. The most popular is No. 4. Smaller numbers (such as 1 or 3) mean sharper curves; larger numbers (such as 6) are for a layout where the turnout is required to branch into a broader curve.

There are also curved turnouts, right and left. When one of these is included in a curve, it will enable your train to turn right (or left) into another curve, or *spur*. It usually isn't as reliable as the straight turnout, however, and you are not advised to include one in your layout until you have become familiar with the regular turnouts and their idiosyncrasies and learned how to adjust them when necessary.

The same is true of another type of turnout called a *slip switch*. This can be used when two sets of tracks (designated A track and B

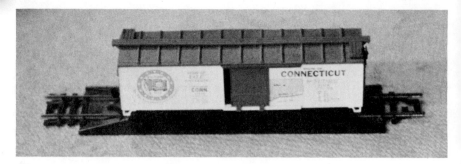

A rerailer section of track helps align the small wheels on the rails.

track) are running parallel. It will permit a train running in either direction on A track to switch over to B track, and one on B track to switch over to track A, again from either direction. It really is as complicated as it sounds, and although it's a joy to behold when trains are passing through it smoothly, unfortunately it can become unexpectedly uncooperative, causing derailments. Reserve its use for the time when you have become more experienced.

The rerailer section of straight track has been mentioned previously; a portion of the railbed between the rails is raised equal to the height of the rails, as are sides of the railbed, on each side of the rails. It resembles a highway crossing, for which it is often used by modelers. Its main function, however, is to help you position the loco and cars correctly on the track. Often when you place an HO or N car on the track you can hear one or more of its tiny wheels clattering against the ties when it moves, meaning the wheels aren't running on the rails. But if you place the car on a section of track adjacent to a rerailer, you can just run the car onto the rerailer track; its construction will automatically bring the wheels onto the rails in correct position.

There are also sections of tracks called *crossings*. These are used when you want one track to cross another at the same level. You even have a choice of the angle of crossing. There are crossings for 90 degrees, 45 degrees, 30 degrees, and so on.

When laying your first track, be sure it is on a flat surface. Then there will be less worry about twisted and loose rail joiners. Hills and trestles are nice but need some extra consideration. First make a circle of the tightest curvature you plan to use and make the final test of your locos on it to be sure they'll operate satisfactorily on it. Avoid

The 90-degree right-angle crossing. These crossings also come in a number of other crossing angles.

BACHMANN HO GAUGE TRACK

1758 90° CROSSING

BACHMANN BROS., INC., PHILADELPHIA, PA. 19124
MADE AND PRINTED IN HONG KONG

running your locos at top speed. You may enjoy watching them race around the track but it's hardly authentic operation; their prototypes never raced like that, except, perhaps, the "Old 97," which ended up in a wreck. On your railroad, you're apt to have a derailment, too.

When you're putting tracks together or adding onto those that come with a train set, avoid a pitfall that all model railroaders are prone to, at least until they learn better. In the vernacular, it's called fudging. When you're completing a course of track and the two ends won't connect because they don't line up or are just a wee bit too short, the tendency will be for you to stretch them a little so they'll meet, or to twist a curve a little sharper or broader.

Be warned that won't work! Oh, it might seem to, at first, if you've cheated only slightly, but eventually your train will derail. Stretching

This crossover is used when the track must cross a brook, highway, or another track.

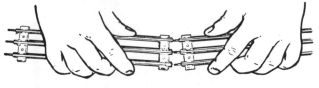

The three-rail Lionel track sections fit together with large pins for rail joiners.

will loosen rail joiners somewhere along the line, and after a train has pushed past them several times, the two tracks will part. Twisted curve sections will kink sharply where they join and that will throw off your loco if the sections don't separate first to cause a derailment.

With all the pieces of short track available—you can even cut your own with the razor saw—and all the different curvatures of track you can get, there's no real excuse for fudging, which at most might save you a trip to the railroad store but will eventually mess up your railroad.

There's another kind of turnout a train modeler may find of use in his layout. It is the *wye* turnout, shaped approximately like a Y. With the regular turnout, the train can continue straight ahead or can be shunted to the right (or the left). With a wye, the train can't proceed straight ahead but can be turned to the right or left with the use of the same turnout. There is still another type of turnout, which gives the train a choice of going to the right, or to the left, or proceeding straight ahead—it's a sort of combination of a regular turnout and a wye. However, you will have to search far to find such an arrangement on a real railroad. Also, the modeler will find it can be quite temperamental and should best be eliminated from his layout; it derails unless it is in perfect adjustment.

8. ARCHITECTURE

BUILDINGS COME READY MADE. Bachmann, for example, offers some beautiful ones. They're less expensive, however, when you purchase them in kit form and assemble them yourself. Many of these kits will be displayed at your railroad hobby shop, and the shelves will be loaded with many more. But better buy carefully, choosing only what you would like to have for your pike. Otherwise you might have so many attractive constructions you won't have room for your trains; and instead of pursuing a model train hobby, you will spend all your time making miniature buildings.

If you have passenger trains, you will want a passenger station or two, and also a freight station. Freight trains carry commercial products to and from factories, and so you will want a few factory buildings. Later you can position them on your layout so you can back up the freights on one or two spur lines of tracks, fed from the turnouts from your main line. A water tower will improve a remote section of track—steam engines need water in real life. Undoubtedly, the factories will be on the outskirts of a town, so you will need private houses and stores and such not too far from the railroad station.

A picture of the completed building is shown on the cover of the kit. You're taking a chance when you buy a kit in a box that isn't sealed; a piece may accidentally have fallen out and become lost. Tell the salesman you're a beginner and check your selection of kits with him to make sure they are simple enough for a beginner. Don't be fooled by the statement on some kits that reads: "For 8- to 12-year-olds." I've seen some of these kits on which the notice should have read: "For 8- to 12-year-old geniuses."

Bachmann's assembled and landscaped farm scene, complete with barn, yard, and animals, comes ready to be installed on your pike.

Tyco's remote-controlled freight unloading depot.

Bachmann's assembled split-level house.

At home, open the box on a table and read the instructions for assembly carefully until you understand them thoroughly. Then try fitting the parts together without gluing them. Don't throw away a piece that seems to be extra and doesn't fit anywhere. You'll find the right place for it; check the diagram. Try to foresee problems before they occur. For example: "window glass" is usually a piece of clear plastic that you cut into oversize rectangles (one for each window) from a large plastic sheet and glue over the window frames from inside. Obviously, if you glue on the roof first, you'll have to reach the inside from the bottom. The bottom is open on many buildings, but windows are easier to position when you can reach inside the house from both top and bottom. Some houses also have shades on their windows.

The buildings are of colored plastic; if you don't like the colors, and you won't in most cases, you can paint them. If you do so, choose gray, brown, beige, or some other subdued color, not a gaudy color. When was the last time you saw a factory painted bright red, green, or yellow?

Front: Bachmann's ready-to-use lighted passenger station.
Rear: Lighted freight station.

Paint is applied with a small artist's brush or from a spray can. Unfortunately not all railroad colors come in spray cans. A large assortment of fine railroad paints is offered by Floquil. And they are inexpensive. Your hobby shop stocks them. Whether you paint them or not, you will want to touch up your model buildings with weathering spray to take away their new appearance.

When the plastic kits become too easy for you, as they will in a surprisingly short time, try one of the Campbell kits. It also is prefabricated, mostly of wood, with some delightfully realistic accessories: signs, wooden barrels, benches which you must assemble, shingled roofs, and many others. A little more care and work, but the results are worth it. These kits must be painted after assembly.

Don't be discouraged if your first building shows your inexperience and ends up looking like something from Li'l Abner's Dogpatch. Put it to one side. Someday you might expand your railroad to include a line into hillbilly country. The first time you climbed on a bicycle you probably ended up on your back, but you soon learned the trick of keeping your balance. You'll soon learn the do's and don'ts of building-making, too.

Not all models have floors or bases. When the model has a floor with grooves into which the bottom edges of the walls can be glued, the building can more easily be shaped with squared corners and will keep its shape till the glue is dry; this can be an advantage.

If you desire, you can glue your model building to a piece of Homosote, but don't fasten it to your layout until you decide definitely where you want it and what landscaping you will want for it. Just stand it on the layout in an approximate position.

Now you have the trains, tracks, and a general idea of a layout and the buildings that will be on it. In chapter 11, we'll start putting your pike together.

9. PAINTING AND DECORATING

FOR MODERN TRAINS, CARS, AND BUILDINGS, a special paint is required for coloring miniatures. A regular paint, thinned down so it could be efficiently applied to small models, would be much too thick and bumpy when dry, and the models would lose their authentic appearance. One of the leading producers of special paint for modelers is Floquil-Polly S Color Corp. Floquil paint covers completely, dries quickly, and when dry, is undetectable except for its realistic color. It comes in thirty colors, all authentic railroad colors. These can be mixed to form an infinite variety of shades.

They can be applied a number of ways. One of the most common is by brush, but since you'll be applying this miniature paint to miniature models, it follows that you should use a miniature brush so it will be applied evenly without streaking. For this purpose an artist's brush is best. It also follows that the paint should be applied in miniature quantities.

Model railroad stores sell Floquil in 2-ounce bottles and brushes of different sizes. The larger sizes are satisfactory for the larger surfaces of your models, but you will need a fine brush for such small areas as a window frame or a post. The thinner for Floquil is Dio-sol, available where the paint is sold. Use it to wash the brush after use. A hobby shop may not have Floquil railroad colors, only Floquil military colors, for hobbyists who make military models such as tanks, planes, and ships, but these are almost the same colors under different names. The dealer will have a Floquil chart so you can choose the colors you desire. The Instant Weathering paint is available in a spray can.

A surface to be painted usually needs a small amount of preparation so the paint will adhere and not flake or rub off when dry.

Porous surfaces, such as paper, wood, cardboard, fabrics, and fiberboard (Homosote), need no preparation. They have many pores to anchor the paint securely. Plaster, if you used it for your hills and mountains, also has pores, but it has too many of them. It will absorb paint like a sponge soaks up water. There are a number of ways to treat the plaster so it isn't quite so absorbent. One of the simplest ways is first to paint on a mixture of 70 per cent Floquil Glaze and 30 per cent Dio-sol—but don't apply it until after the plaster has dried thoroughly (about two weeks). Put on several coats of the mixture without waiting for the previous coat to dry. Then wait two weeks and paint with the desired color. If you've used wallpaper paste and strips of paper towels, it requires the same treatment.

A, B, and C are the primary colors. A and B make green. For orange combine B and C. For brown use B and C and black; for dark brown add more black. (Floquil-Polly S Color Corp.)

Before being painted, wood should be sandpapered to remove all marks and finally finished with very fine steel wool. Rub the steel wool in the direction of the grain of the wood. Wipe the wood with a cloth dipped in Dio-sol to remove all dust, and let it dry.

Nonporous surfaces such as metals, glass, and plastic have no pores to hold the paint. But often a metal surface will be covered with microscopic pits and scratches that will hold the paint. As a test, paint a small portion of the surface, let it set a week, and then try to rub it off. If it adheres firmly, probably no treatment is necessary. If you don't want to wait that long, carefully wipe the metal with fine steel wool. This will provide many tiny scratches to which the paint can cling. In any case, before painting the metal surface, wipe it with a cloth soaked in Dio-sol to remove all grease and oil.

Many plastic items can be painted without preparation. An exception is a plastic known as styrene. An object molded of styrene is easy to recognize: when struck with a pencil or screwdriver, or when dropped on a wooden table, it gives off a metallic sound. Styrene plastic is vulnerable to Dio-sol, the solvent in the Floquil paint, and is apt to crack or "craze" (become misshapen with running colors), when exposed to large amounts of it. This is important to remember because many railroad cars and scenery items are made of styrene. The remedy is first to paint the plastic with Floquil RR19 Barrier, a liquid that contains no Dio-sol and does just what its name implies: it gives the plastic a barrier coating to protect it from the Dio-sol in the paint. Barrier takes one hour to dry thoroughly. It must be thoroughly dry before you can apply colored paint.

If an item requires more than one color with the second color overlapping or touching the first, let the first color dry three days so the Dio-sol in the second coat of paint won't dissolve it. Also, when painting an unassembled building, be sure no paint runs onto an edge which must be glued against another edge; the paint might prevent the glue from holding. If you should accidentally paint one of these edges, you can wipe off the paint with a cloth dipped in Dio-sol. The same is true if you accidentally get any paint on the track rails, where it might form an insulation preventing the loco wheels from making electrical contact.

To prevent running and streaks or brush marks on the finished surface, immerse no more than half the brush tip in the paint, and apply with even strokes in only one direction; don't brush back and forth or try to work the paint into a porous surface such as wood. After three days you can apply a second coat, but this is seldom necessary. For striping locos, cars, and scenery, a special striping wheel is available; it lays on the stripe just as the special striping machine paints white lines on a highway.

In your painting projects, you will find Scotch Magic transparent tape is often a decided help. Use it to fasten paper shields over areas you want to protect from the color you are applying. To make a stripe, apply two strips of tape separated by the distance you wish to be the width of the stripe. Then paint the open area between the strips. You needn't try to make straight lines; the edges of the tape will provide a straighter edge than you could possibly make by hand. Remove the tape as soon as possible after painting. If the tape has been attached to a previously painted surface, when removed it will not disturb this paint, as long as the surface was prepared before painting and the paint was given at least three days to set permanently.

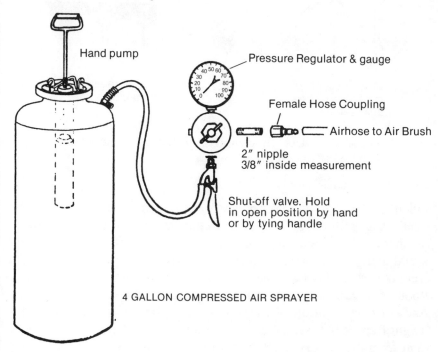

Hand pump

Pressure Regulator & gauge

Female Hose Coupling

Airhose to Air Brush

2″ nipple
3/8″ inside measurement

Shut-off valve. Hold
in open position by hand
or by tying handle

4 GALLON COMPRESSED AIR SPRAYER

Compressed air sprayer, for airbrush. It's less expensive but bulkier than a regulation airbrush outfit. (Floquil-Polly S Color Corp.)

Another method of painting, one used by many advanced hobbyists, is with the use of an airbrush. This involves blowing a fine mist of paint on the object by means of compressed air. The result is free of blemishes and looks very professional. The difficulty with this technique is that a special tool that includes a small air compressor is required, and it can be one of the most expensive items in the hobby. It's nice to have, but it is costly.

The subject of weathering has been mentioned previously. At one time railroad modelers enjoyed having their trains, buildings, streets, and houses looking spick-and-span brand-new. But this appearance is most unlifelike. Paint fades in time, due mostly to sun, rain, and snow. Trains are subject to mud, dust, and grime as well. You can simulate fading by adding a drop or two of white paint to your color before painting.

The accumulation of mud, grime, and dust can be simulated very effectively by a spray can of Instant Weathering available from Floquil. A quick spray on the object is sufficient. The original color is

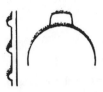 

Cross section of   Rust   Side of model showing
car showing how   spot.   grime deposits.
dust settles.

Cross section of car showing how dust, rust, and grime
collect. (Floquil-Polly S Color Corp.)

still there but now it looks honestly weathered. But don't apply the weathering without giving consideration to what objects should be weathered and how much. A house in a forest may be faded but would almost never have been subject to grime or dust. Its foundation area, however, may be subject to mud, spattered up from heavy rain. Roofs of buildings in industrial areas are affected more than the sides. And—a consideration often overlooked by modelers—all cars in a freight train aren't weathered to the same degree. One may look new, right from the factory; another old-timer may appear much the worse for weather-wear. If you can visit a railroad line in your vicinity, watch a freight as it rolls by, and take some photographs for later study. You'll find all cars have different degrees of weathering.

Unless you're exceptionally talented, your first painting project will not be one you'll boast of, but you'll be amazed how quickly you'll learn. Soon, with a fine brush and some red paint, you'll be putting rust on freight-car hinges. There are many other possibilities that will occur to you. Any mistake you make, you can always paint over.

If you desire the appearance of woods for a suburban station platform, a house porch, or some such, Floquil also makes realistic stains (Flo-stain) in oak, maple, pine, and others. They can be applied with a brush or wiped on with a cloth. They will also add special color to a brush-applied weathering solution you can make from the old Dio-sol you used to clean your brushes.

Floquil comes in small inexpensive bottles. Some other colors beside Instant Weathering are available in spray cans, such as Grimy Black, to simulate locomotive soot; Coach Green, and Reefer Yellow. A complete booklet on this subject, titled *Painting Miniatures,* is published by Floquil-Polly S Color Corp. Your railroad shop may carry it.

There are other railroad paints, of course, but the above brand is easy to use and most popular among modelers.

10. LANDSCAPING

YOUR TRAINS ARE RUNNING AROUND YOUR PIKE, through turnouts and past buildings and towns (at least rudimentary ones), and you are getting a great deal of pleasure from them. Then one day you notice that something is missing. Finally you realize what it is. You have a flatland railroad. And no matter how realistic your trains and buildings are in appearance, they are in a toy-train world. Your pike needs landscaping to give it a final touch of realism. This means adding a mountain or two, some hills, perhaps a lake or stream, a tunnel beneath a mountain, some trees, shrubbery, lawns.

Some mountains and hills can be purchased ready-made at your hobby shop and can be fitted into your layout, but these prepared ones will not be your handiwork, and you will have to work hard on them to disguise the fact that they came from an assembly line. You'll be much prouder of the scenery if you know you built it with your own hands. This isn't difficult to do.

A word of caution—if you have dreamed of having your train climb a mountain, you had best forget it. It has been mentioned previously that a model loco engine's power does not necessarily determine how many cars it can pull. When the load is too heavy, the loco's wheels will simply skid on the tracks because it is too light to give the wheels sufficient traction. This also is true if you try to have your loco climb a steep grade, even with a load of only a few cars. In real life a loco is never required to climb a very steep grade or even a low mountain. It might make a circular course around the mountain, climbing gradually, or may make a gradually sloping climb across the side of the mountain. The rule of thumb for model railroads is about a 2-inch rise in about 10 feet of track. Most often you can climb more steeply than this, but by all means try the grade first before anchoring your tracks permanently.

Some modelers run their pikes on two levels, one at least 1 foot below the other. To enable a train to climb from the lower level to the upper level without having it climb gradually along a straight track over 60 feet long requires an unusual setup. At one end of the upper and lower platforms, a wooden structure like a shallow spiral stairway must be erected. Tracks are laid on this gradually ascending spiral. The curvature of the tracks must be large enough to be safely negotiated by the locomotive—usually an 18-inch radius.

The train on the lower platform climbs along this spiral and thus reaches the track on the upper platform. A similar arrangement is used for a descending train. Since such spirals are not found on full-size railroads and so are very unrealistic, they are not landscaped or decorated and are hidden, perhaps by a curtain; they aren't boxed in solidly, however, because they must be accessible in case of a derailment or breakdown.

Mountains and hills are often made of plaster of Paris, which can be formed to create a realistic appearance, but which has its faults. It hardens quickly, sometimes, in dry weather, too quickly for the inexperienced. And it is subject to improper drying and distortion in high humidity. It chips and cracks easily. There are other materials only slightly more expensive that are somewhat slower drying and more durable. One of these is common wallpaper paste, available at most paint stores.

First a form is required. For a hill, this can be as simple as a crumpled newspaper. Set it in the desired position on the layout and then stretch a piece of heavy paper over it; a piece of a paper shopping bag will do. Tack or staple the edges of this paper so they lay flat on the layout. Next, be sure to cover any adjacent tracks or buildings to protect them.

The wallpaper paste can be mixed in any convenient bowl or tray, such as a discarded ice tray from a refrigerator. Mix it to the consistency of heavy cream. Then dip in it inch-wide strips of paper toweling, one at a time, and lay them on the paper form so they overlap slightly. Apply at least six layers of these paper strips, and cover the entire form. Finally, with a trowel or large spoon, cover them completely with the paste.

Train running through the lower tunnel, which is unfinished—portal hasn't been installed as yet. The larger the mountain, the more impressive it will be. (A & D collection)

It takes about two hours to set in dry weather. Before it dries, press in slightly with your finger to form hollows where you think they might add realism. Squeeze the surface slightly between two fingers to add bumps and ridges. A very small pinch of sand here and there will resemble rocks. A small piece of gravel will be a huge boulder.

When you've made a hill and have discovered how easy it is, it's time to tackle a mountain. There's nothing that adds more interest to a pike than the sight of a train disappearing behind a mountain, then reappearing on the other side, unless it is the sight of the train entering a tunnel under the mountain, then continuing out the other side.

A mountain is made in the same way as a hill but a firmer supporting form must be used. This consists simply of a frame made of wood or Homosote cut to become vertical supports. Imagine that the mountain you have in mind is miraculously made of cheese, and that you've cut it vertically from top to bottom in parallel cuts every 10 inches of its length. Your Homosote supports will be similar in shape and position to these imaginary slices.

Many hours went into building this mountain range and the Gettysburg battlefield. (A & D collection)

If you plan to have a tunnel, cut appropriate holes to take the tracks at the bottoms of these forms. Glue their bases to your railroad platform. For covering the top of your mountain, you can use strong paper from a shopping bag, stapling it to the tops of the Homosote forms. Many modelers prefer window screening to paper; not only is it stronger but it can be bent and dented to resemble more realistically the uneven surface of a natural mountain.

Caution—when handling this wire screening, always wear gloves, otherwise the sharp edges will cover your hands with numerous cuts. Screening is available at hardware stores. It comes curled up like a scroll. First flatten it out and curl it in the opposite direction so it will be easier to handle. Bend its surface sharply here and there to cause fissures, and bend and twist it slightly so it will lie more realistically and form gullies on the mountain. Staple the edges to your pike table and cut off the excess.

Portals for your tunnel, entrance and exit, both for single tracks and double tracks, can be purchased at your railroad shop. The better ones will look as though they have been made of cut stone. Cut your mountain covering to allow the insertion of these entrance and exit

This Amtrak is on time. Note the coal pockets in the yard and the tunnel detail. (A & D collection)

portals. Before "plastering" your mountain, be sure the tracks under it are covered with paper to protect them from the occasional spot of wallpaper paste that might drip through the screening; this paper can be removed later through the tunnel openings. Obviously, it's not good practice to have a turnout under a mountain, unless you have made the mountain easily removable, or with an open back, set against a room wall where it won't be noticeable. Most derailments occur at turnouts, and such an accident under a mountain where it is inaccessible can be a real problem.

Cover the mountain form with three or four layers of towel strips soaked in wallpaper paste as you did when making a hill. Use a trowel or your fingers to make imperfections in the final covering layer of the paste, or stipple it with the ends of a large stiff-bristle brush if you have one handy; after all, there are no perfectly smooth mountains in nature.

Here are some tips. When covering your hill or mountain with wallpaper paste-soaked paper strips, soak each strip separately and apply. Some modelers prefer laying the strips in crisscross design instead of parallel. When the last of the strips has been applied and it's time to

This and opposite page: Bachmann's ready-made trees—all kinds for all seasons.

cover them all with the paste alone for a finish, don't spread it on but slap it on in gobs from a soup spoon; the result will be an uneven and more realistic appearance. Also make slashes in the finish with the edge of the spoon to simulate gulleys, ridges, and cliffs. Since wallpaper paste dries more slowly than plaster, it's best to let your hills and mountains stand a couple of days before doing any further work on them.

If you want your hill or mountain to be removable, build it on a large sheet (or on two joined sheets) of waxed paper. Then, when dry, it can be lifted off easily. But use care! You won't be able to staple the edges of the paper or screen covering flat on your pike base, of course, but you want these edges to be thicker, anyhow; if they're too thin they'll crumble easily during removal and replacement of the mountain.

Mountain grass can be simulated with green paint (see chapter 9), but you'll get a better effect if you use artificial grass, available at your hobby store. This is nothing more than green-dyed sawdust.

Paint the place where you want grass to "grow" with a thin coat of Elmer's glue. Then put the grass in a large kitchen strainer and shake it on the glued spot. When it's dry, in about an hour, blow off the excess.

Your store also sells artificial trees—maple, oak, pine—in winter and fall colors. Some brands are better than others; check several before buying. When your hill or mountain is dry, drill a small hole and insert the tree trunk. Don't glue it in place; you may want to reposition it later. Shrubbery and small evergreens are positioned similarly.

For a lake or stream, use glossy blue-green enamel. Most railroad modelers agree that the only glossy part of a pike layout should be the water. Put on the enamel in a thick coat so it runs. When dry, it will appear like running water. With the edge of a spoon, some modelers are able to give the wet paint the appearance of ripples. Your hobby shop sells ready-made lakes, too. One of these might tempt you. They're quite interesting and real looking.

Few modelers use real water on a layout because of the danger of

You can begin enlarging your pike from a simple circle or oval by adding a large or small siding. But avoid reverse loops or at least recognize one when it occurs—it requires special wiring.

rust to a valuable piece of equipment. As an experiment for my pike, I perfected a real waterfall and river but I never let my trains near it. The waterfall ran off a mountain into a small lake at one end of the layout. The water ran down a river to the other end, then dropped into a plastic container. From there it flowed back through a plastic tube under the layout to a reservoir below the base of the mountain at the other end. From there it was lifted back to the waterfall by an air-lift pump, the kind used by tropical fish fanciers to circulate water in an aquarium. The beds of the "falls" and "river" were painted blue-green and covered with pliofilm from a dry cleaning bag.

Artificial lakes and rivers provide the railroad modeler with an opportunity to use interesting trestles and bridges. If a train derails and falls into artificial water, there's no harm done—unless the drop is a long one.

Grass lawns for a suburban house are made just like the grass on the mountain—with glue and green-dyed sawdust. There also is artificial earth which you can sprinkle on glue to form country dirt roads. (Real earth won't work; it's much too coarse.) Pieces of cardboard, cut to shape and painted black, are best for macadam roads. Paint the cardboard a buff color for a concrete highway. You can't use toy autos for these roads because their scale is too large, except on an O gauge pike. Specially made autos in HO and N scale are available at your hobby store, as well as all sorts of figures—vacationers, workers, and trainmen, and dogs, horses, and cows. Good figures are expensive because of the work involved in making the fine detail.

For a highway RR crossing you can use cardboard roads leading up to the track and away from it, with a smaller piece between the rails. A section of rerailer track makes a very satisfactory crossing.

Even if you put cork roadbed under your tracks (see chapter 11), they'll still look not quite like a real track construction. With a little patience and work you can remedy this fault and make them look more authentic. Notice the roadbed of real railroad tracks; it is gray or yellow-brown gravel. Ballast for your model railroad tracks is also available in these colors at your hobby store. The way it is applied is similar to the way you "grow grass."

With a small brush, apply Elmer's glue to the cork roadbed between the ties and at the sides of the track. Then sift on the ballast (either gray or yellow-brown—your preference) with a strainer. When it is dry, brush off the excess with a dry brush. Don't worry about any specks of ballast that fasten on the ties themselves; this adds to the realism. A road crossing (rerailer) needs no ballast. And it's best not to ballast a turnout; if you feel you must, use *great care*. Stray particles may interfere with its action and possibly jam it.

One last decorating suggestion—you may have a beautiful pike with wonderful, realistic trains and landscaping, and just behind your prize mountain is a wall covered with flowered wallpaper, or a garage wall of boards. Such a setting effectively destroys realism. The best solution would be to have an artist paint a scene on the wall showing distant mountains and a lovely blue sky filled with whipped-cream clouds; or, if the wall is behind a model industrial city, a booming factory town with smoke drifting upward from its factory smoke stacks.

Unfortunately most of us are incapable of such works of art, nor can we afford to hire someone who is capable. But there are compromises. If you have permission to paint the wall, a light blue color will create the illusion of distance. Use any brand of flat indoor paint. Also, companies in model magazines advertise large murals. One of these, mounted on a large piece of Homosote and hung on the wall behind your pike, will be effective. Large stationery stores sometimes sell these murals. Before buying one, be sure the scenery on it isn't too large for your small-scaled landscaping.

The safest scene is a cloud-filled sky. If there is an urban or woodland scene below the sky, perhaps when the mural is mounted this part of the picture can be lowered so it is concealed from view by your pike table.

If you're confident of your artistic skill, you might try making your own trees. A dry Y-shaped twig (not a green twig) will serve as an old battered winter oak or maple. You can make trees of twisted strands of wire, with some of the strands bent outward to resemble branches. Paint them gray. And from the ends of the branches hang lichen, a live, spidery long-lasting type of growth common to the Arctic regions (your railroad store can get it for you). It comes in green for summer or evergreen foliage, and brown for fall. Or you can dip a bunch of it in Floquil paint for the desired color. When you have finished decorating, examine your trees from a distance of about five feet. With a little imagination, you'll swear there are little leaves growing from those wire trees.

SECTION III

PLANNING YOUR PIKE

The Atlas *Selector* is a convenient electrical switch combination. Each Controller can shut the power off or turn it on in each of four blocks.

11. YOUR TRACK LAYOUT

YOU HAVE A LARGE CHOICE OF TRACK PLANS. Bridges, trestles, tunnels, and other features can be added later. One precaution:
avoid a *return* (or reverse) *loop,* at least until you learn some wiring
tricks. A return loop occurs when a train completes a loop that directs
it back onto the same track on which it entered the loop. It is not an
impossible situation but it requires special wiring. Think about it a
minute and you'll understand why.

When your loco comes into the loop, the right rail is live. When it
leaves the loop and enters the same track from the opposite direction,
the left rail (on its right side) must be live, otherwise the electrical
current will be passing through the loco in the opposite direction
causing it to stall. Obviously, an arrangement must be made to
reverse the current fed to the loco, when it returns to the original
track, so it will continue without hesitation. This reversal is amazingly
easy to accomplish and I'll explain how in chapter 12.

If your track layout butts against a wall or other obstacle so you
can't walk around it, make sure its width is small enough for you to
reach across to the farthest side without smashing a nearby building
or derailing a train on the near side. In any case, the turnouts on the
far side should be remote-controlled, if only for convenience.

Near turnouts can be manual ones, since they'll be easy to reach. In
my first pike, the far turnouts were manual. I used a long stick to
reach their levers to turn them—not exactly a prototype operation
and also a pain in the neck; I soon replaced them. Even if you can

walk around your pike base, it's still a nuisance to make that walk every time you want to operate a turnout.

If you plan to operate more than one loco on your railroad, you will want at least one *siding*. This is a length of track that runs off your main line from a turnout, parallels your main line and then enters it again through another turnout. Its value is obvious. It provides a track on which you can park a slow train such as a freight, or park a passenger train at a station, while the faster train continues past it on the main line. Then the slow train continues after it.

Spurs, which are dead-end branches from your main line, lead to freight stations, factories, and commercial sites. A train on a spur can't continue ahead and reach the main line. The loco or switcher parks it in front of the loading platform, and returns later to pick it up. Special dead-end sections of track are available; each carries a bumper, lighted by a small red bulb, to stop a car and keep it from running off the end of the track should it go too far.

Your plan needn't be a closed circuit in the shape of a circle, oblong, or something similar. On a narrow shelf running the length of your room or along two walls of your room, you can plan a "point to point" pike from Doodletown at one end to Toonerville at the other. The simplest way to bring back your train after its one-way trip might be to uncouple the loco, turn it around, and hook it up again. But you'll have to transfer the current to the other track to make the loco head the right way; this will be easy to do by flipping a switch that you can easily wire into your control panel. Operating the reverse lever on your control pack (if it has one) won't do it; the loco will back up no matter how it's pointed. Later you might use a second loco to bring back the train, or turn the loco around on a turntable; these arrangements would be a more realistic operation but might be too tricky for you as a beginner.

The main advice you should heed when planning your first pike is *keep it simple*. After looking over a copy of *Model Railroader* magazine, or visiting a local club layout, or gazing at the pike set up at your railroad store, your impulse will be to arm yourself with a ton of supplies and then try to put together something resembling the old New York Central, Union Pacific, or "Chessie" (Chesapeake & Ohio) lines—a layout that the most skilled veteran would hesitate to attempt. An oval track, and a couple of turnouts for a siding will serve to initiate you into the hobby and give you a feeling of accomplishment. When you expand, do it one step at a time. You'll adopt various little tricks, manipulations, and priorities.

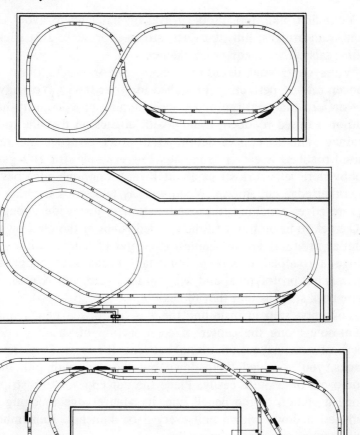

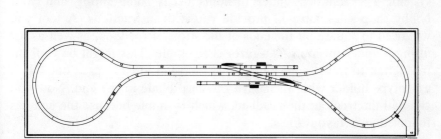

Four suggested layouts by Minitrix (Model Power). The black identifications at the side of the track represent the turnout control. Black indicators in the center of the track show optional uncouplers.

Your first pike, too, should travel on flat land to avoid complications—no bridges, hills, culverts, streams, or such. Just stick to fundamentals till you acquire confidence.

With your layout determined and your tracks in place, you can concentrate on perfecting a roadbed for your tracks. You have probably noticed that real railroad tracks running cross-country have been laid on a raised roadbed, usually with ditches on the side to facilitate drainage and to collect debris so it won't obstruct the rails. This raised roadbed is easy to simulate. For example, for HO gauge your hobby store sells cork strips about 1 yard long, one edge beveled and the other edge cut square. When you lay two strips together with the square edges touching, the combination is just wide enough for an HO track to fit on top with the beveled edges of the cork on the sides. Similar products are available for N and O gauges, although for O gauge a roadbed is not as important because O gauge three-rail track is not prototypical and will still look artificial. A nice feature of these cork strips is that they're flexible.

Your first step in installing them is to draw a pencil line on the Homosote along the center of each section of straight and curved track of your layout, marking between the ties. Then remove the tracks; you've nailed them down but the nails will pull out of the Homosote base quite easily. Place the flat edge of one strip of cork along a section of the pencil line, its square edge touching the line, and nail it down with a nail every 3 or 4 inches. Remember it will bend around a curve quite easily.

Next butt the square edge of another strip of cork tightly against the square edge of the first strip at the center line and nail it down. Continue until you have installed the roadbed for your whole track system. The roadbed under turnouts needs some fitting and your hobby shop salesman will provide you with instructions. A tool you will need to square off the ends of the strips of roadbed, as well as for fitting it under turnouts, is a razor-sharp knife. This might be your introduction to the X-acto knife, if you haven't already used one—it is a pentype holder with a small razor-sharp blade in the end. Now you can nail the track to the roadbed, which is simple because the bed has followed your layout lines.

The cork not only adds realism to your layout, but also deadens the toy-train clatter of your cars as they run the rails, resulting in a more true-to-life rumble. Clatter can be especially annoying if you built your pike on plywood instead of Homosote. In a very large layout, plywood may be used beneath the Homosote to help stiffen it, although it does make wiring more difficult when wires must be run up through the base to reach accessories that require electricity.

Next, set your buildings in place. Don't anchor them in place because seldom will the positions you give them at first become their permanent sites. You'll find you'll soon be shifting them as new ideas occur to you. Also, railroad tracks are seldom on raised roadbeds as they pull up to a station or a factory. The solution is not to cut out the roadbed at these positions but to elevate the facility to the height of the roadbed. If you have your building on a piece of Homosote as a base, you'll find that this elevation is just about right. Merely cutting out the roadbed will cause slopes and grades which will twist the track sections and give you trouble.

Undoubtedly, as you become more and more experienced in railroading, you'll be rerouting tracks as well as changing building sites in attempts to make your pike look as prototypical as possible. Your problem is not only to fit your railroad into the small area you have available (for HO, even 8 by 10 feet is small), but also to make your trains appear to be traveling a long distance. Hills, mountains, rivers, highways, and so forth, can help create this illusion. Parallel tracks can be separated by buildings, rows of trees, or low ridges to prevent them from appearing too close. But realize that, for the sake of authenticity, mechanical features such as bridges and tunnels should have reasons for existing, i.e., a bridge must cross a chasm or river, a tunnel must go under a hill or mountain. At first you'll put them in your pike just to add interest, but eventually you'll add features that will make an observer believe that you have to have them in order for your train to negotiate the terrain.

In my 4 by 8 foot HO pike, on the left end I had a mountain that extended 3 feet toward the right onto the table. A tunnel entered at the far side and exited from the near side. But under the mountain I had two curved sidings, both leaving the main line under the mountain and rejoining it before it left by way of the exit tunnel. On both sidings I parked freights with their own locos. I would send a passenger train into the tunnel, stop it on the main line, and bring one of the freights out of the tunnel exit. The impression was that the passenger train was still on its way to Timbuktu, and that the freight had just come from there. The parked trains, of course, were not visible to

Power packs that come with train sets are usually quite simple, which keeps down the cost of the entire set. You'll find yourself graduating to more sophisticated controls such as those produced by MRC. Here is one of their Railine units.

an observer. The turnouts under the mountain had to be remote-controlled—and the mountain was removable, so the maneuver was no problem.

Now that you're setting up your pike on a permanent basis, still subject to alteration and expansion, of course, a point may be mentioned that you've become aware of already—if you own cats. The little trains zipping around fascinate them. My male Burmese-Manx loved to crouch behind a building, hoping to be unseen, and as the HO train passed, he would reach out a paw and pat it, frequently with enough muscle to derail it. Then he would wait patiently until I put it back on the track and it came by again. When I sent it off on a siding, he would stretch his neck in wonder, then return to his waiting position.

A smaller female cat preferred the N railroad. She would run after the train, knock it off the track, and try to carry off one of the cars in her mouth.

All very cute and fun to watch if you have the patience and love cats. Some of their actions were amazing. I once made a tunnel from a shoe box for an O layout. There was just enough room in it for the big train to get through. A large red cat I had at the time saw the train coming and scurried into the tunnel from the far end. Much to my amazement, the big train entered the tunnel and came out the other side without hesitation. How the cat managed not to block the train in the tunnel has always been a mystery, even after I encouraged a number of repetitions of the feat, examining each as closely as I could. I never discovered how the cat had the magical ability to permit two objects to occupy the same space at the same time.

Be warned never to leave cats alone with your pike. They find buildings, especially the valuable wooden ones which are the most difficult to assemble, fun to chew on. They also love to sleep in a long tunnel under a mountain. A forest of trees is also a nice place to curl up after some have been chewed.

12. POWER
FOR YOUR PIKE

THE BASICS OF WIRING YOUR RAILROAD are simple and easy to understand. Even when your pike becomes larger and more complex, the actual wiring will remain simple (thanks to the manufacturers who supply easy-to-follow instructions with their accessories). But you'll need a great many wires. The main problem is identifying the wires and being sure that the correct one is hooked up to the correct terminal. Wire a small pike first so you can appreciate the manipulation that will face you in a large one.

To run your model railroad you must use a power pack. A simple one is supplied with most railroad sets. The power pack for O gauge is essentially a transformer that reduces the 110-volt current from the wall outlet to a smaller voltage current that can operate the alternating-current motor of the loco. A rheostat on the power pack enables you to feed this electric current in varying amounts to the track and from there to the loco to regulate its speed. The power pack for HO and N gauges is slightly more complicated. The motors for locos of these gauges use direct current, so the pack not only reduces the 110-volt house current to 12 volts, but also rectifies it from AC to DC.

The better power packs in HO and N, such as those made by MRC, not only provide 12-volt DC current for the trains but also 16-volt AC current for the accessories such as lighted buildings and turnouts. DC current is more suitable for the HO loco; AC current for the accessories, because they require more power. To avoid any drain on

One of the most advanced power packs is the Tech II by MRC. It permits almost perfectly realistic operation of your train—slow stops, idling power, and no jackrabbit starts.

the HO loco's current that would lessen its efficiency, speed, and control, the power sources are separated. The terminals on the power pack are clearly marked. Don't confuse them. If you mistakenly connect the AC terminals to your track, you'll burn out the DC motor on your HO or N loco.

With a special terminal track section in your layout, which sometimes comes in the form of a rerailer, connecting the two wires from the DC terminals on the power pack to the track is simple. If you don't have such a terminal track, you can purchase two terminal wires from your hobby shop; these are wires with rail joiners soldered on one end. These rail joiners, each attached to a wire, replace those you have joining two sections of track. Just fasten the other ends of the terminal wires tightly to the plainly marked DC terminals on the power pack and your train is ready to roll.

A short circuit can occur when a metal object, such as a screwdriver or a metal locomotive or car, lies across the rails, allowing the full force of the current to travel down one rail, across to the other, and back to the power pack without doing its work turning the loco motor. The train won't move, of course, and if such a short circuit is allowed to continue, it can damage the power pack. In the MRC power pack, a red light will glow and the pack will automatically shut off in the event of a short circuit, thus protecting the pack from damage. When the problem has been corrected, the light will stop glowing in a few minutes at the most, and the pack will be ready to

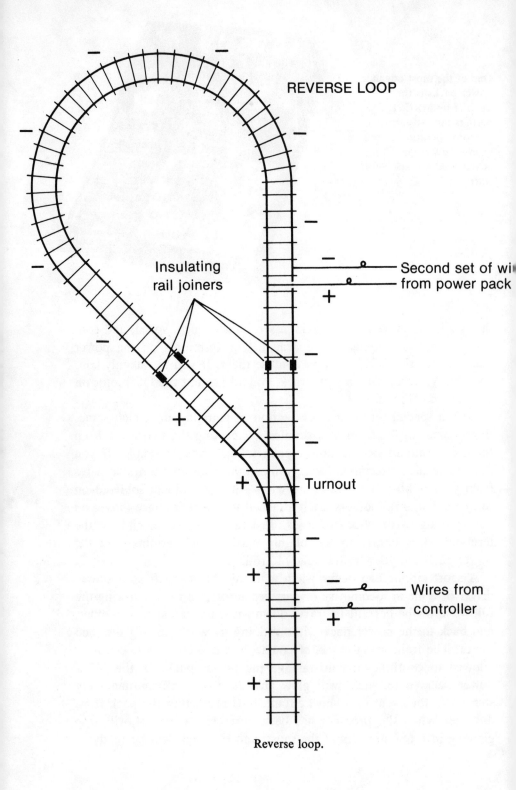

REVERSE LOOP

Insulating
rail joiners

Second set of wi
from power pack

Turnout

Wires from
controller

Reverse loop.

operate once more. If the cause of the short circuit can't be immediately found and corrected, disconnect the pack until you find and remedy the fault.

If your pike has more than one remote-control turnout or other electrical accessory, it may be best to connect your AC terminals on the power pack to a terminal board available at the hobby shop. This is a simple device with two rows of terminals, one on each side. A wire from the AC connection on the power pack is connected to one side and electrifies all the terminals on that side. A wire from each accessory is connected to a terminal on the other side of the terminal board. The return wire from each accessory will run through its on-off switch to a similar terminal board connected to the other AC terminal on the power pack, completing the circuit. This is a better arrangement than running a bundle of wires from the power pack.

The wires from your accessories can be run to the terminals on the terminal board and each accessory will have its own terminal.

When connecting the switches from the turnouts to this board, follow closely the directions which are supplied with each turnout. A caution when using the remote turnouts: just a momentary depression of the switch will operate a turnout. Its "motor" is rather delicate. It will be seriously damaged if the switch is held in contact. If the turnout doesn't snap to a new position, maybe you have pressed the switch lever the wrong way.

If the switch is pressed correctly and the turnout still doesn't operate, don't keep pressing the switch; the trouble is elsewhere, probably a loose wire—or else the turnout motor has already been damaged. A problem you will have, at least at first, is remembering which way to press the turnout switch to direct your train straight ahead or to the turnoff track. Bachmann turnouts will help you remember; the switch of each has two small lights, a red one for a turnoff and a green one for straight ahead.

Switches for other accessories are generally more simple. Connections can also be made to your terminal board. The type of switch used by many modelers is the toggle switch. Atlas Tool Company makes a variety of excellent simple switches. Tyco's horn comes with a press-button switch so that you may sound it briefly, at intervals, in the manner of a real train.

Now meet a new type of rail joiner—plastic, and therefore an insulator, it interrupts the flow of current along the rail. It is used in a system of control called the *block* system. For example: a freight train pulls off on a siding to let a fast express go through on the main line. Something must be done to keep the freight on the siding until the main line is clear. The tracks of both the siding and the main line are electrified. A block must be established on the siding to interrupt the electric current and halt the loco that's on it.

To do this, insulate the last two sections of track that connect the siding to the turnout that brings the freight loco back on the main line. Insulate just one rail by replacing the metal rail joiners at each end of the rail of the two sections with joiners of plastic. Keep the metal rail joiner in place on the rail between the two sections of track on the insulated rail. Now the current will not be able to flow from one rail through the motor and back along the other rail. When the loco reaches that insulated double section of track, it will stop.

Now it won't ride through the turnout and crash into the passenger train. But we have another problem: how to start the freight loco moving again after the passenger train has passed. This is done by putting electricity back into the insulated double section. First check which rail you have insulated, the right or the left. Then go back to your power pack and check which terminal of the pack the wire connects to this rail. From that same terminal connect a wire with a soldered metal rail joiner on its end to the two insulated track sections; simply put this wire-connected rail joiner in place of the one that connected the two insulated rail sections. Now the effect will be the same as if you had not insulated the rail.

When the loco reaches the double section, current will flow through the motor back to the power pack. The loco can go. To adapt this system so you can control it, simply put an on-off switch into the wire that runs from the power pack to the insulated sections. Turn the switch off and set the turnout into the siding; the freight train will turn into the siding and its loco will automatically stop when it reaches the insulated sections. Turn the turnoff back so the oncoming passenger train will continue on the main line. When the passenger train is safely on its way, turn the turnoff ahead of the freight loco to bring it back into the main line, flip the switch to feed current to the insulated sections, and the freight train will obediently go through the turnout and follow the passenger train.

The block system can be used to advantage on other parts of your pike, especially if it is a long one with many turnouts. It is advantageous wherever you want a train to stop automatically, such as before going through a critical turnout, or on a siding, or in a rail yard.

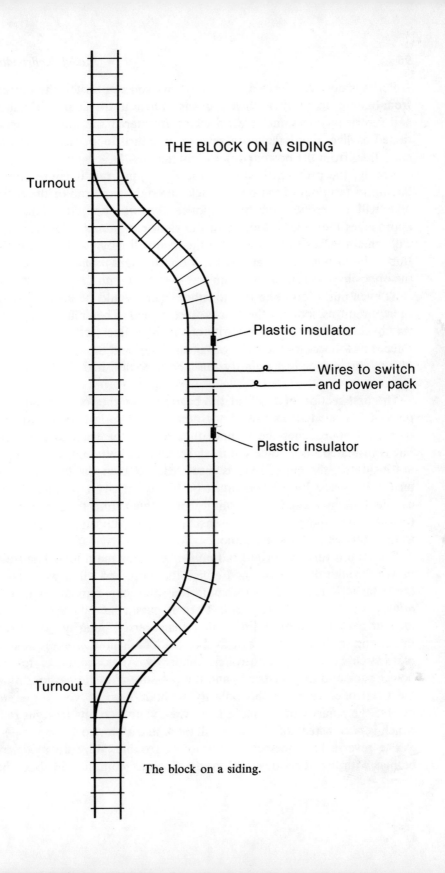

THE BLOCK ON A SIDING

Turnout

Plastic insulator

Wires to switch
and power pack

Plastic insulator

Turnout

The block on a siding.

Perhaps now you have a hint as to how you can switch the current from one rail to another when you want a loco to travel around a loop and return on the same line on which it entered the loop. As mentioned earlier, this is called a reverse or return loop. Insulators and extra lines from the power pack supply the answer.

Simply, the problem is this: if the right-hand rail is connected to the *minus* terminal of the power pack, the right-hand rail of the entire pike will be *minus* and the opposite rail will be *plus*. The loco approaches the reverse loop with the right rail *minus*. The right rail will remain *minus* in the loop and the loco will move with no trouble. But at the turnout at the end of the loop, the right *minus* rail becomes the opposite *plus* rail of the main line—and *this can't be.* In fact, you can't even put a loop like this together; there would be an immediate short circuit as soon as the tracks were joined. The solution: on the way back, reverse the rail polarity of the main line (left rail to *minus* since it now becomes the right rail of the loco, and the opposite rail to *plus*). This reversal of polarity must be accomplished at the correct time.

The first section of track at the beginning of the loop beyond the turnout is insulated, as previously described. The last section of the loop as it approaches the turnout that returns the train to the main line is insulated, too. Since the track sections at both ends of the loop are insulated, the entire loop is insulated. To keep the train moving on the loop, the loop tracks must be fed electricity separately. This can be done by using a wired rail joiner running from the power pack to some convenient spot on the insulated rail, with an on-off switch, as in the block setup just mentioned.

The loop is turned to right rail *minus,* as in the main line. The train passes through the turnout and enters the loop, and all is well. Then the polarity is reversed on the main line; the loop remains right rail *minus,* which the loco requires. Then it passes happily through the turnout back to the main line which has reversed polarity (right rail in relation to the direction of travel of the loco is now *minus*). A simple switch called the Controller, made by Atlas, connects to the power pack and to your track, and the pressure of a sliding button on the Controller reverses the polarity without fuss. If you forget to reverse the polarity of the main line, when your loco hits its right rail, which is *plus* instead of *minus,* it will buck like a bronco.

The reverse loop seems to be a lot of trouble. Why do modelers bother with it? The description may sound complicated but the

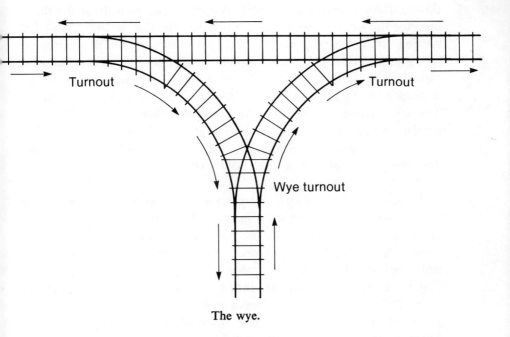

The wye.

wiring really isn't. A word of advice: be sure the loop is long enough to hold your entire train and that the whole train is on the insulated track before you change the polarity of the main line, otherwise you will cause a short circuit. As for the value of the reverse loop, it is one of the easiest ways of turning a train around without removing it entirely from the track. It also takes less space than any other method.

Another turnaround method is called the wye; it uses a wye turn-out, a left turnout, and a right turnout. The train turns right on the wye, then enters the curve of the right turnout, pulls entirely through it, then backs up straight through the right turnout and straight through the left turnout. When the entire train has passed through the left turnout, it pulls ahead, taking the right curve of the left turn-out and the other branch of the wye, which puts it loco-first on the main-line track once more, but headed in the opposite direction (see illustration).

It's like turning an automobile around by turning into a driveway, backing out in the opposite direction, then turning to drive forward in the direction from which you came. Of course, a long train requires quite a bit of track at the ends of the right and left turnouts. And as for the reverse loop, insulation (also called *gapping*) of certain sections of track is necessary, as well as a change of polarity of the main line, for the same reasons as in the reverse loop. A simple device for turning around usually just the loco is the *turntable*. The uncoupled loco and its tender pull onto a circular turntable. The circular table is turned completely around until its tracks, carrying the loco, are aligned with the tracks on which the loco approached the turntable. The loco leaves in the opposite direction when the turntable has turned completely around. Gapping and a change of polarity is needed here, too. The turntable is turned by a small electric motor. This device is available at your hobby shop, too, but it is among the more expensive items.

As you can see, electrical switches—to operate a turnout, turn lights and blocks on and off, operate a horn, drawbridge, and other accessories—will accumulate as your pike grows. You must have some centrally located easy-to-reach place to put them, such as a control panel. Rarely is a railroad table a good place to mount them; they may be activated accidentally, but most important, there will seldom be room for them. You can make your panel of a 1-foot by 1-foot square of Homosote. Glue narrow strips of Homosote under the side edges to elevate them so there will be room for the wires beneath it. Mount your switches with the screws provided with them and, near each switch terminal, punch a hole in the Homosote panel with a screwdriver or ice pick so the wires can be passed through to the bottom of the panel. Under the panel these wires can be attached to a terminal bar with each pair of terminals insulated.

Wires from the accessories can be attached to the corresponding terminal on the terminal bar. This is a rough design upon which you can elaborate as you see fit. Your train's power pack can be placed on your railroad table if there's room for it, or else on a small separate panel attached to the table, preferably on your right side (if you're right-handed). The control panel with its switches can be attached to the edge of the table on the left, where you can operate the switches with your left hand.

Some modelers prefer to paint their control panels before fastening down the switches. A popular color is dark green (paint from Floquil), sprayed or painted with a brush. Some modelers use a panel large enough to contain a complete diagram of their pikes. If such a diagram is wanted, the panel is first painted white and allowed to dry. Then ½-inch strips of Magic tape are applied to indicate the course

Bachmann's freight yard set.

of the tracks, narrower tape is used to show sidings. The easiest way to do this is to apply a long strip of tape, then cut it to the right length on the panel with an X-acto. The excess tape can then be peeled off after all the tape is in place; the entire panel is painted green, and when it's dry, the tape is removed. The result is white tracks on a green background.

All switches on the panel should be marked with labels so you can identify them quickly.

On an elaborate pike, you will have a maze of wires that can be most confusing. If you are a beginner, even the few wires on a small pike must be surely identified if your wiring is to be successful. For example: a remote-control turnout 4 feet away will require two pieces of wire at least 5 feet long; identify these wires. Identify every wire at both ends with a tag of transparent tape on which you have written in ink the number of the switch or turnout, or the name and location of the accessory, and the terminal of the accessory to which it connects. If you make a wiring mistake, which all of us do at first, the tags will also help you trace wires and connections.

For wiring more intricate arrangements such as wye turnarounds, turntables, and accessories, a complete, easy-to-understand and inexpensive pamphlet titled *How To Wire Your Model Railroad* can be obtained at your hobby shop or by writing to the Atlas Tool Company.

Wires from the control panel to the accessories should be run under the Homosote surface of your pike and extended upward through holes in the Homosote at the required positions. Hold them to the bottom of the Homosote with transparent tape. Running these wires on top of the table will clutter your landscape.

Wires come with insulation of various colors, notably red and green. Note the colors, such as red for the current to a turnout and green for the return. You can't have too much identification. The first time you experience any problem, you'll know why.

13. PIKE ACCESSORIES

IT IS LOGICAL THAT MANUFACTURERS who have mastered the technique of producing authentic scale-model locomotives and cars should apply their techniques to track accessories that operate as realistically as possible—freights that do more than just run on rails, railroad buildings that function according to their purpose, remote-controlled drawbridges. There are a multitude of them, and the number you can use depends entirely on the length of your pike. Some operate completely automatically. There is even an electronic system that permits trains to "sense" each other's approach, the proximity of road crossings and similar potentially hazardous situations. The only difficulty with it is that the railroad modeler must be an electronic engineer (or almost) to install it.

Tyco, which makes the remote-control steam whistle in a billboard, offers over two dozen other accessories. One is a gravel conveyor that carries gravel from a side storage bin to a hopper car via a conveyor belt. Another is an operating gold mine; it conveys gold ore from an overhead bin to a dump car (hopper) which, in turn, dumps the ore into a trackside bin located at another part of your pike. Then there's an automatic highway crossing gate; the gate lowers as the train approaches the crossing, rises when the last car has cleared the crossing, and has flashing lights. The piggyback loader-unloader loads and unloads trailer bodies on a flatcar by means of a crane. There is an automatic highway crossing with a guard: when a train approaches, the shanty lights up and the guard appears with a lantern; he goes back inside the shanty when the last car of the train leaves.

Bachmann's operating log car with dump station.

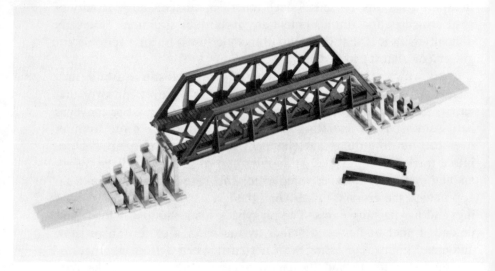

Bachmann's bridge and trestle set.

Bachmann offers a highway crossing with automatic gates, blinking lights, and a bell. For diesel pikes, there is a trackside oil storage tank containing a realistic diesel horn. There's a remote-control bascule (lift) bridge for one track crossing above another: when the bridge is open, the train on the upper track automatically stops, then starts again when the bridge is lowered; when the bridge is lowered, the train on the lower track automatically stops, and it starts again when the bridge is raised. There is also an operating caboose with a mailbag pickup platform: as the caboose approaches the platform, a mailman opens the caboose door, steps out, takes the mailbag from its hook, reenters the caboose, and shuts the door. Quite lifelike! Bachmann also offers an operating log car with separate dump station; Tracksters, which are scale-size models of a Ford van and a Jeepster both with train wheels—Tracksters are miniature inspection vehicles that can travel your pike along with your trains.

Model Power and a number of other manufacturers make similar operating accessories. Lionel offers an assortment of interesting ones in O gauge. The best way to discover what is available is to request a catalog from each company.

A working accessory that will add tremendous interest to your pike is a turntable. This was mentioned previously as an easy way to turn a loco around so it will head in the opposite direction. Probably its main use, however, is to *feed* locos into an enginehouse.

An enginehouse is a building in which locos are serviced and repaired. It consists of a number of stalls, each with a pit below the tracks so the loco can be reached from below, similar to the service pit in an auto repair station. The engine fronts on the turntable and is curved to fit the circular turntable. Each stall, of course, has a piece of straight track which butts against the turntable so the straight track on the turntable is aligned with it when the turntable is turned to the desired position.

A turntable is a necessity when the enginehouse consists of three or more stalls. Otherwise, a jumble of tracks and turnouts would be required to direct the locos to the stalls.

There are two problems with a good remote-controlled turntable. One is that a good one is expensive. The other is that the motor operating the turntable fits below the surface of the pike; this means that there must be space for it below the pike. If you have constructed your railroad on a piece of Homosote, as suggested, you must raise the Homosote sheet by placing wooden blocks beneath it at numerous

Bachmann's remote-controlled lift bridge.

The Stationmaster contains electronic speaker. Operator of train speaks into microphone.

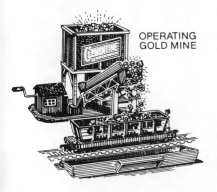

OPERATING
GOLD MINE

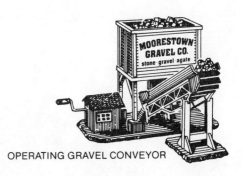

MOORESTOWN
GRAVEL CO.
stone · gravel · agate

OPERATING GRAVEL CONVEYOR

Tyco's operating gold mine.   Tyco's operating gravel conveyor.

places, being sure the Homosote won't sag in spots from the weight of the trains and accessories on your pike. This elevation will have other advantages. With the extra space below, you will be able to sink your lakes and rivers below the surface, which will add to their realism. You will need this space, too, for the Kadee remote-control uncoupler which fits below the track.

In operation, with the remote control you turn the turntable so its track lines up with the incoming track, run the loco onto it so it fits completely, then with your control turn the turntable so its track and the loco line up with the track leading into the desired stall.

As you surely realize, a blocking system is required to insulate the stall tracks so the locos within won't go barging out the back of the enginehouse or come backing out the front whenever you turn the throttle on your power pack. Make sure that complete wiring instructions come with your turntable when you buy it. Incidentally, Campbell Scale Models offers an enginehouse kit containing two stalls. It is very authentic, with simulated stone-block wall construction. Two of these kits will give you a four-stall house. Don't attempt this kit, however, until you've had some experience assembling the more difficult constructions.

Don't overlook the cassette tape recorder as a railroad accessory. With it you can tape the sound of a real train rushing along the track, the sound of the loco, and other authentic noises. Unfortunately, you'll have to travel far to capture the *chug* and *whoosh* and steam whistle of a steam loco, since these old-timers are few and far between, but the diesel and its horn are common. You'll be amazed how these true-to-life sounds will make your little train a true-life experience for you as it goes around your pike.

Tyco's automatic crossing gate.

Even a small pike can be landscaped to arouse the admiration of your friends.

The miniature cassette recorder is the best because it can fit inside a building. (Leave the top of the building removable so you can remove the recorder to adjust its controls and change the cassettes. The subdued thump of disco music coming from Mabel's Cocktail Lounge in Bumpkinville will make your visitors rub their ears in astonishment.

Campbell makes a country church kit, complete with "stained-glass" windows. One modeler made part of his pike as a module; that is, he could remove this section of his pike, including its scenery, and replace it with another module. In this way he changed the seasons, shifting between winter and summer. His winter module contained the church, and it and the surrounding scenery were covered with snow (from a spray can). During the Christmas season, a small recorder within the church played carols. The sounds of the carols issuing from the church's open doors was extremely effective. (He said he had a hard time finding a tape of carols with just an organ accompaniment. Finally he went to a local cathedral and recorded the choir.)

14. MAINTENANCE

YOUR MODEL RAILROAD won't require much maintenance if you don't abuse it, but the small amount it does require is important if you want to avoid serious future problems.

The small electric engine in your loco is a delicate instrument. Avoid subjecting it to dust, dirt, or moisture. It is essentially an armature, consisting of wires wrapped around a metal core, which is attached to a shaft. This armature is centered within two arms of a permanent magnet. When electric current is fed to the wires, the armature and shaft rotate rapidly. When the shaft rotates, a gear at one end turns another gear system connected to the driving wheels of the loco, making them turn and thus moving the loco.

Around the shaft near the armature is a series of small copper plates that rotate with the shaft. This system of copper plates is called the *commutator*. Two small carbon blocks, one opposite the other, slide against the commutator as it rotates with the shaft. These are called *brushes*. They are held firmly pressed against the commutator by spring arms. The copper commutator is connected to the wires of the armature. One of the brushes carries the incoming electric current, the other the outgoing current. The small plates of the commutator are insulated from each other so the current has to go through the armature.

To summarize: the current from the live rail travels along an insulated wire to one brush, then through the commutator to the armature, and out the other brush to the loco body, where it meets the other rail and returns to the power pack. The commutator is so wired to the armature that while it rotates, although the brushes are always changing position on the commutator, there is a continuous flow of current through the armature. Note that the locomotive must be insulated from the incoming current from the live rail. In some locos the current is picked up by a metal shoe which is attached to the insulated wire coming from the brush and which rides on the live rail either before or behind one of the wheels. In other locos, one set of wheels—usually the wheels on the right side of the loco—is insulated from its axles and the body of the loco and serves to pick up the current, transferring it to the commutator brush. Watch for this when you assemble a loco from a kit; follow instructions carefully. In other models, the tender of the loco will serve as part of the circuit.

One end of the armature shaft fits into a small bearing in which it turns. There is a second bearing through which the shaft fits and turns; this is usually located between the commutator and the drive gear at the end of the shaft. This bearing and the end bearing support the shaft and keep it in line. These bearings are the only places where friction and wear can occur; these are the only spots which need oiling, and then *very little*. If neglected they can wear so much that the shaft wobbles, and then you will need a new motor. The brushes may eventually wear or corrode, but operating produces only slight friction on them, and they can last for many years.

The armature turns because current passing through it generates a magnetic field that is not in alignment with the magnetic field of the permanent magnet. The armature turns to assume a position that will place the magnetic fields more in alignment. As soon as it turns slightly, the brushes touch another pair of plates on the armature and the current in the armature is changed, which alters the position of the armature's electric field again, causing the armature to turn again. This is repeated over and over again, resulting in a spinning motion of the armature. Your only maintenance of the motor, therefore, is to place one tiny drop of oil on the bearings.

Oil applied to any other parts of the motor or its assembly can cause trouble because it can interfere with the flow of electric current and can even interrupt this flow by acting as an insulator. The drive gears are nylon and need no lubrication. The loco's drive wheels turn on shafts which rotate in bearings on the loco body; these bearings should also have a drop of oil. Apply oil to the bearings of the motor about once every ten hours running time; oil the wheel axle bearings about once for every fifty hours. The oil is an especially thin type sold by your hobby shop. A special applicator, also available at the shop, enables you to pinpoint one drop at a time.

You are not advised to disassemble the electric motor; reassembling one is a job for experienced fingers. Motor bearings can be reached fairly easily in most cases. Sometimes a bottom plate must be removed from the loco's body to expose the motor; sometimes the bearings can be reached through the loco's cab.

You probably have heard that at one time owners of new automobiles were advised to drive them slowly for the first thousand miles or so before operating them at top speed. (No more; the theory now is that the sooner the bearings wear out, the sooner expensive repairs will be necessary, and this keeps repair shops busy; or maybe the owner will even buy a new car, promoting sales.) But we don't want our loco motors to wear out prematurely. So it is best to "break them in." Run them slowly for the first twenty hours or so before you run them at top speed. Actually, you should never run them at top speed if you want them to operate like their prototypes; you are not racing cars. A tiny steam loco whizzing along a track at top speed would be traveling the equivalent of 200 to 300 miles per hour for the prototype, which never happened.

Freight and passenger cars need no particular oiling or maintenance, but working cars, such as those that unload logs, open doors, or dump gravel, might. Check the instructions that came with them. The same advice applies to working accessories such as automatic crossing gates, and semaphore signals, etc. But *never* oil an electrical contact.

Turnouts need no oiling; they don't operate long enough or often enough for friction to be a factor.

Unpainted metal parts that aren't depended upon to make electrical contact, such as car axles and wheels, periodically can be wiped with a lightly oiled rag to discourage rust.

Tracks cause the most common trouble. An oxide builds up on the surface of the rails and interferes with the passage of electricity between them and the loco body. A special liquid, available at your hobby store, is the antidote. Apply a little of this track-cleaning fluid to a cloth and rub the top of the rails; it dissolves the oxide. You'll know the rails are oxidized when the loco skips or falters and doesn't travel smoothly. Use the liquid sparingly. If only one section of track subjects your loco to this faltering, rubbing its rails lightly with an ink eraser can also solve the problem.

Model Die Casting makes a special inexpensive track-cleaning diesel. The flat bottoms of four posts, mounted two at each end of the diesel, ride the rails as the diesel moves. The original idea was to glue pads of sandpaper to the pylon bottoms so they'd brush the rails and clean them, but I tried a different method successfully. At the pharmacy I bought a thin felt pad, the kind with adhesive on the back, used for bunions and sore spots on the human foot. I cut four circular pieces and stuck them to the pylons. On the two in front of the diesel, I put a few drops of the track-cleaning fluid. The rear two I left dry. As the loco moved on the track, the front pads applied the liquid and rubbed the rails; the rear pads wiped off the excess liquid and finished the polishing. After one trip around the pike, the rails sparkled. I had to replenish the liquid on the pads only once, about halfway around. Rubbing the rails by hand with a cloth might have been as fast and perhaps even more thorough, but at least my way was closer to the "prototype way."

If your loco bucks and falters even on clean tracks, usually the least likely cause is the motor of the loco. The most likely cause is faulty track joiners. A friend tells me he never has any trouble with his track joiners. He says the reason is that he replaces all joiners with new ones once a year.

Perhaps all joiners needn't be replaced, but they should be inspected at the first sign of trouble. They tend to loosen, sometimes mysteriously. And when they do, there's incomplete electrical contact between the rails. A few modelers, with lots of time on their hands, solder the joiners to the rails, making a sure, durable connection. When, with experience, you consider yourself a soldering specialist, this might be the way to go. The only problem with it is that you have the extra job of unsoldering when you want to add to or subtract from your pike.

The problem with joiners is that they're rather fragile, and a slight pressure can open them. When this happens, the remedy is to remove the joiner and carefully squeeze it back to its original shape with a sharp-nosed pliers. This is a pair of pliers with its jaws almost pointed at the ends. It is handy for doing delicate work. While removing the joiner, you probably twisted the track section and loosened the rail joiners at the other end, too, so inspect them as well.

Inspect also the wires running from the power pack to the rails. A terminal track section, available in some sets, facilitates the attaching of wires from the power pack to the tracks. The plugs at the ends of the wires from the power pack simply plug into sockets on the track. If you have a terminal track section, the plug-in terminals may have oxidized; clean them with fine sandpaper or emery paper. Sometimes the fastening to the power pack can loosen. The bare end of the wire, twisted, should be wrapped around the projecting terminal in a clockwise direction. Then the thumb-screw is fastened tightly on top of it. This seems simple, but an apparently tight connection can be deceptive. You've fastened it tightly, perhaps even with a pliers; but sometimes a single strand of the multiple-strand twisted wire can insert itself along the terminal shaft and be caught under the finger-screw. This makes it difficult to turn the screw, so you think that the screw is tight against the wire when it isn't.

The single strand will serve as an electrical connection for a while, but soon it will snap as the wire is accidentally moved during use, and the connection will be broken. Before completing the connection, twist the strands tightly together and be sure no stray one projects. Then bend them around the pack's terminal so they follow the direction of the screw when you tighten it. This is easy to check: if the twisted strands unwind and spread when you fasten the screw, they are placed with their curl the wrong way. That is, the screw turns clockwise as you tighten it, and the twisted strands should be looped in the same direction around the terminal. Multiple-strand wires may seem to be a nuisance in this regard, but they have definite advantages.

The above precautions should be taken when making any electrical connection with them, even with screws. Even when you can apply the force of a screwdriver, the strands can untwist and spread. Near other terminals, a stray strand can even reach another wire and cause a short circuit.

When an electrical accessory stops functioning, the chances are that a bad electrical connection is the cause.

The power pack needs no particular maintenance, except for the wire connections mentioned above. Of course, be sure the DC terminal is connected only to the tracks and the AC terminals only to the pike accessories. If your pike is a brand-new one, check this *before* you run your first train.

The landscaping and architecture of your pike require no special servicing except for the periodic removal of dust, which will accumulate in spite of your best efforts to avoid it. It's true that a certain amount of dust might make buildings more realistic, but it has no cosmetic effects on trees and shrubs or on the shining surface of an artificial river or pond. On the tracks it can be sucked up by your loco's motor. How to remove the dust? A friend thought he had a perfect and simple solution—a vacuum cleaner. It removed the dust, certainly, but also most of the trees, shrubs, and ballast from the tracks' roadbed.

There's a better solution. Small battery-operated vacuum cleaners, as advertised on TV, are sold by novelty stores and large pharmacies. They are very disappointing for housework because they don't have enough suction power. Not enough for rugs and upholstery, perhaps, but just enough for a model pike. If it still seems to be too weak, use a soft brush in one hand to dislodge the dust, and work the small vacuum cleaner with the other hand to remove it.

With action accessories such as *roundhouses* (enginehouses) and drawbridges, maintenance instructions are usually included with the product. The same is true of action cars.

Repainting is seldom required unless you become tired of one color and prefer another. Most wear marks of the paint, such as scratches, can be considered "character marks" and don't detract from the appearance of your pike. Buildings can be repainted according to instructions in chapter 9. A newly painted side or roof of a house or building, or panel on the side of a freight, can pass as a real repair in the prototype world.

When you've finished running your trains and decide to leave your pike for the day, disconnect your power pack from the wall socket to protect any accessory you may have accidentally left turned on. At least, you'll keep bulbs from burning out prematurely. Don't let pets have access to your pike when you're not around to protect it. The Tyco steam-engine whistle mounted on a billboard is activated by a flat button in a small receptacle that fits on the control panel. One modeler taught his pet terrier to step on the button to turn on the sound. Great fun! Until one night he forgot and left his power pack plugged in. About three o'clock in the morning a *whooo-hoooo* sound echoed through the house. The dog, all by itself, was showing its skill. No harm done except some loss of sleep. But if the tricky little terrier had accidentally exerted some prolonged pressure on one or more of the remote-control turnout switches, it would have seriously damaged the delicate turnout mechanisms.

SECTION IV

YOUR
RAILROAD EMPIRE

15. PERFECTING
YOUR PIKE

YOUR PIKE IS COMPLETED and your trains are running beautifully. It needs just a few finishing touches before it can be called an empire. One of them is that it should be run as a *real* railroad, which includes your running it as an engineer.

The first thing you will want is an engineer's cap. This may seem a nonsensical, trivial thing, but ask any advanced model railroad buff about the importance of a cap. When you put one on, a magical change seems to take place. No longer are you just a hobbyist running a miniature; you become a real engineer operating a real railroad. Notice the pictures of other modelers in the railroad magazines. Almost every one of them is wearing an engineer's cap. These caps are sold inexpensively at the railroad shop. Usually each has a line emblem in front of the crown, such as NYC for New York Central; later you can change this emblem to the name of your own line.

Your empire should have a name of your own choosing. If you have patterned your pike after an active railroad, that name should certainly be on your loco or its tender. The emblems are available at your hobby shop. They aren't decals but transfer letters, which are even easier to apply. However, large mail-order retailers sell them as decals, also. They sell large catalogs listing hundreds of names from which you can order. Individual transfer letters, also available, must be used if you make up your own name.

My railroad was the Ratlum Mountain Railroad. Each letter had to be put on the loco tender separately. Care had to be taken to apply

them in a straight line. I cheated a little bit—I abbreviated "Mountain" to "Mt.," but this is permissible. You'll also need the decal catalog to get names for your towns, passenger stations, and sundry places, such as stores and offices which should have names. When purchasing names, be sure you specify the gauge of your railroad so the lettering will be to the correct scale.

Of course your railroad should operate on a schedule. For example, a passenger train pulls into "Barkville" at a certain time, leaves two minutes later, and arrives at "Treeville" a half hour later. Obviously, actual times can't be used on your scale railroad since distances are reduced and the time it might take your HO train to travel from one station to the next would be only a few seconds. You can stretch it by having the train make two or more complete circuits of your pike before stopping at the second station, but this is no complete solution. A clock on the wall that races ahead half an hour or more per second would be a help; I have heard that there are such clocks but I have never seen one. A stopwatch and a little restructuring of time can be to your advantage.

Modelers have different ways of solving the problem. With the stopwatch, count the seconds it takes for the train traveling at a slow, realistic speed to reach Treeville station from Barkville including two circuits of your pike. Let's say this time is sixty seconds on a short pike. Choose a convenient scale, one easy to use, involving multiples of ten—such as, ten seconds equals half an hour; then sixty seconds

If your pike is ultramodern, it should have a *Metroliner* running the rails.

would be three hours. Use this scale on all your trains, passenger and freight. And chart all your trains. Remember that you will have perhaps a fast passenger train, an express, and a slow freight. Time them and add each train to your chart.

From this, make a schedule: it should contain the names of the stations and the trains' arrival times. Then add a schedule for the freights with the depot names. An "ex" after the time can denote an express passenger train or a fast freight. Since a slow freight will have to pull into a siding to let a fast passenger train have the right-of-way, the arrival time at the turnout might also be included for the information of the engineer or engineers. Remember that the times will all be based on the converted clock you have chosen, in this case ten seconds equals half an hour. The schedule will begin like this:

Town   *Leaves:*
Barkville   1:00
Treeville   4:00 (Note: sixty seconds later)

If you have a drawbridge or some other accessory that might delay the train, this delay need not alter your schedule. Trains can be late in the real world, and often are. It is a good idea to date your schedule; you might add a train or a station that would make the old schedule obsolete. Duplicate the schedule and give copies to your guests and other engineers who might be helping you handle another one or two of your trains.

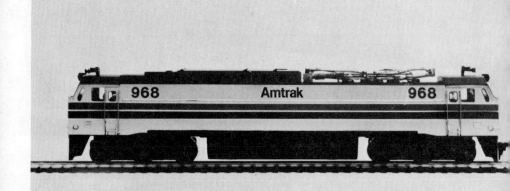

Another touch of the modern is the Amtrak *E60CP.*

How can another engineer handle a second train on your pike? With a separate panel he can control the block system over which his train passes and perhaps also the pertinent turnouts. For example, he can work the turnout into the siding when the fast passenger train is behind his slow freight, and he can disconnect the block that insulates the track section at the end of the siding that causes the freight loco to stop automatically. When the passenger train has cleared, he can restore current to the block and turn the second turnout so the freight can continue on the main line. Of course, after the freight has cleared to the main line he must remember to adjust the turnout back to the main-line position in preparation for the next through train.

Turnouts are designated by numbers or capital letters on the diagram of your pike drawn on each control panel.

As mentioned in a previous chapter, it is virtually impossible to have a cornfield collision between the trains. Turning the loco around on the track will simply make it back up. In other words, all locos will run only in the same direction unless designed or altered to do otherwise. The simplest of these alterations—*to be attempted only by a modeler with considerable experience with loco motors and considerable manual dexterity, or one with an unusual desire to see locos wreck each other*—is to disassemble the motor and reverse the per-

A magnificent pike is the one designed and constructed by Adolf Arnold, famous train collector and owner of the A & D Toy-Train Village and Railroad Museum. This layout is 22 by 22 feet. On it, fifteen trains run at the same time. The mountain in the background is 10½ feet high.

manent magnet, thus reversing the poles and making the armature spin in the opposite direction.

To make your railroad even more authentic, you might decide to have tickets for your passenger train service. You can pass these out to visitors who come to see your pike in operation. Tickets should be free; die-hard modelers enjoy showing off their trains to an audience. The usual cardboard ticket is the size and shape of the ordinary small card that printers have in stock because they are the cheapest to produce—a factor, since you will have to pay to have them printed. On the card should be the name of your railroad, the type of train, and the destination. For example:

RATLUM MT. RAILROAD
Destination: Treeville

Express coach
We specialize in delightful scenic trips
through the wonders
of the Evergreen and Ratlum Mountains.
Refreshments available
Price: $150 one way

If you include refreshments, you probably will have to serve your guests soda or coffee. The price of $150 is, of course, just a gag. Undoubtedly, you can choose wording more suitable to your line and services than that shown above. Some modelers have a side hobby of collecting such tickets from pikes they have visited.

One modeler with exceptional imagination and a feeling for science fiction passes out tickets for a special excursion he schedules through a prehistoric park. The park is a forest just beyond a low mountain. The passenger train, with a Civil War loco and appropriate old-fashioned coaches, wanders back and forth through trees copiously decorated with miniature plastic insects and animals and small replicas of prehistoric monsters. There's even a stop at a forest refreshment stand. He calls his park The Enchanted Forest. Sounds silly, and it is. But I understand that all serious modelers who have "taken the excursion" have admired it, not laughed at it.

There are many legitimate things you can do to add excitement to your empire. Some used by prototype trains are actually unknown to many modelers. For example: the big 4-6-4s of the New York Central, on their way up the east side of the Hudson River to Albany, never stopped en route to pick up water to replenish their big boilers. A section of the tracks above Harmon had a large trough constructed in the center between the rails. This was filled with water. As the train approached the trough at full speed, a scoop was lowered from beneath the engine, and at 75 mph it scooped up several hundred gallons of water in a few seconds. Such an arrangement on your pike, although the loco would not actually scoop up water, certainly would be an unusual conversation piece.

Most people are under the impression that all steam locos were black and that passenger coaches were painted in sedate dark colors.

Germany offers modelers what might be one of the future's first high-speed trains—the *Schienenzeppelin*. The propeller at the rear actually turns. Careless fingers, *beware!* (A & D collection)

Such was not the case. Many locos had silver wheels, or at least silver sidewalls on the wheels. Some locos were colored bright orange, green, or even red, and the coaches were painted to match. The bright color schemes became the trademarks of the railroads and were featured in the lines' advertising, and it was generally thought that the bright colors attracted customers. They gave the railroad train a festive kind of atmosphere. So experienced modelers won't laugh at your train's colors, either. Get a history of the old steam lines from your local library to give you ideas. (See Bibliography.)

If you give your imagination full rein, there are many simple things you can do to make your empire distinctive. At a flaw in a mountain, disguised to look like a cave, one imaginative modeler planted an HO-scale sign that warned: "Beware of Trolls." Eventually every visitor's eye fell on the sign, largely because of its isolation, and when the sign was read, some actually voiced the comment, "Clever." Others just thought so without saying it.

If you have what you consider a high mountain on your pike, spray the top and the trees there with artificial snow, the spray-can type. Toy stores sell kits of interlocking logs and other easily assembled materials that can be used to create unusual wilderness buildings. Near the Tyco billboard with its steam-engine whistle, put a cow (Bachmann makes it) on the track; after much *whooo-hooooing* while the loco waits, remove the cow (unfortunately this must be done by hand) and let the train continue.

Dress up the room in which you have your pike with railway posters and other railroad memorabilia.

Incidentally, be aware that "smoke" for smoking locos comes in three types: odorless; pine scent, if your loco is a woodburner; and bituminous scent, if your loco is coal-burning.

For added interest, set up an N gauge pike to run in a bare area inside your HO layout. It's even possible to lay N rails between the HO rails, but it takes a bit of doing. Not very authentic, but fascinating, nevertheless.

If sufficient space is available, such as an empty garage or hall, contact the modelers in your community and start a railroad club in which everybody chips in time and money, and building the empire becomes a community project. You'll have a large, complete empire in a short time. Each member supervises the part of the operation in which he is most skilled. All members are engineers.

16.   HIGHBALLING
INTO THE FUTURE

SINCE THE RAILROADS THEMSELVES are gradually disappearing from the American scene, in many areas replaced as a means of transportation by aircraft, automobiles, buses, and long-distance trucks, it is difficult to predict any further development of model railroads. Experts prophesy that no new gauge is apt to supersede the HO and N. And the trains themselves have become as realistic in appearance and operation as can possibly be achieved without increasing their cost drastically.

Should a new type of commuter train such as the monorail (a train with overhead wheels running on a single suspended rail) become popular here as it is in a few places in Europe, we may be able to add them to our layouts. Control of model locos probably will become more sophisticated. The control of two or more trains running on the same track still leaves much to be desired, although having an engineer for each loco can be a solution. A few years ago an attempt was made to solve this individual control problem with a system regulating each loco by an electrical impulse to which the loco was tuned, with different impulses for different locos. However, this "solution" was not without its drawbacks. Expense was an important one. Reliability was another. And it was too complex for most modelers.

Radio control is an important next step. It used to be that the only models radio-controlled were model airplanes, but the system has been refined and miniaturized and now a number of radio-controlled model autos and trucks, battery operated, are on the market; and they

One of the first radio-control power packs is already here. By MRC, it can control two trains separately.

aren't as expensive as one would suppose. Watch for radio-controlled locos, or even accessories. The loco will be powered through the tracks as usual, and the radio signal will activate a mechanism that will vary the loco's speed from full stop to maximum and also reverse, duplicating the manual controls supplied by most present-day power packs. With radio control, various other functions could be given the engineer, such as turning the loco's headlight on and off, sounding its whistle, operating signals and crossing gates—no more difficult than controlling the speed of a model car and steering it, etc. In fact, in many ways less difficult.

There's one rather amusing problem with radio control, however, as fans of radio-controlled model cars have recently discovered, which doubtless will influence its use on model trains. The use of a CB (citizens band) transmitter next door or down the block may start your passenger express or freight racing around the track when you least expect it. Other radio-controlled accessories may also start working as if by black magic. A number of car fans have seen their radio-controlled autos mysteriously get up and go all by themselves. It is reported that one radio-controlled model robot started playing music and parading across the floor late one night seemingly of its own volition, and in so doing it scared the wits out of its youthful owner and his family. But these models are battery powered. With a model train you can avoid this CB influence, at least when you're not running your railroad, by pulling the wall plug which supplies power to your pike.

Another development in the not-too-far future is computerized train control, which can be used either with the present standard layout or with one that is radio-controlled. A small computer, which has been programmed with your train schedule, will run your train for you, stopping it at stations, turning it off on alternate routes, and performing all other operations. All you have to do is sit back and watch.

Computers used to be very intricate, complex, and large devices, and it took an electronic engineer to run them. But not anymore. The computer *chip,* as small as a piece of paper confetti, has revolutionized computer technology. It is the "brain" of the modern small calculators. It has made possible all the electronic toys and games which have flooded the market. If you are sold on computers it's a sure bet that one day they will be running your pike for you. They will not only regulate the speed of the train, but also will operate the horn, lights, turnouts, uncouplers, drawbridges, signal crossing gates. Such computerization will not be for me, no matter how fascinating it may be, because it would deny me the pleasure of running the train with my own hands and imagination—the most enjoyable aspects of being an engineer.

Another innovation we might see is the development of a high-speed train. The principal factor that has been the obstacle to actual high-speed trains (150 mph and faster) has been the condition of the tracks. If you've ever looked down a real railroad track from a station platform, you have seen that the rails aren't as straight as they might have seemed when viewed from the side. Not only do they curve slightly from side to side, but they undulate slightly because of variations in the roadbed. If you've ever ridden in a train going 60 mph, you have noticed how the cars whip back and forth. This is partly because of the uneven tracks. They weren't laid by architects but by a crew that spiked them down because they appeared to be straight. Too much whip is very dangerous and can cause derailment. Another factor has been the side play between the wheels and the rails. The wheel flanges do not fit tightly against the rails and the loco and cars can shift from side to side. There are a few really high-speed trains, such as the one in Japan, but its tracks and undercarriages have been meticulously designed and installed so that there is virtually no whip. Turnouts also are as nearly perfect as possible, and curves are gradual and adequately banked, as are the turns of the Indianapolis Motor Speedway.

Your present model train will run along a straight track safely. You don't make a practice of making it do so because it isn't authentic. But you would be operating authentically if American prototypes ran at 120 to 150 mph. Some day they will, if they are to continue to exist and compete with other forms of transportation. Then all you'll have to do is make sure your straight runs are absolutely straight and bank the curves. Of course, to preserve realism, there will be new scale models of the new prototypes. Modern model sectional tracks are actually far straighter than prototype tracks.

The high-speed pike described above would not be a giant step forward in model train development. It would not be much more than a novelty to have miniature trains whizzing along an abbreviated track. If your pike could be 100 feet long and 50 feet wide, it would make more sense. But there is another railroad variation that has been on the drawing boards for a number of years, and someday the major lines may have to put it in use. It not only makes a higher speed possible but also makes the ride more comfortable for the passengers. And it requires less maintenance than current prototype pikes. It requires just a single surface rail. The diesel loco and cars ride on this rail on two wheels each. The train is kept upright on the rail by a gyroscopic stabilizer in each unit of the train. This stabilizer is similar to the giant ones used to keep ocean liners on an even keel in a rough sea. It is really a simple and efficient system, and the railroads probably would have put it to use years ago but they shied away from having to replace their tracks with the monorail and having to junk all their current equipment. It could easily be adapted to models, however, and would make a fascinating ultramodern pike.

For the hobbyist who likes trains but absolutely must have, *right now,* something that runs at high speed, one manufacturer offers a set that includes a combination train layout and an auto raceway. The train pike is assembled on the surface of the table. The raceway is mounted over it on supporting pylons. The operator can have the train running at a moderate speed below, while above it the cars race around their grooved speedway at breakneck speed.

Of course, in the future an increasing number of parts of model pikes will be available ready-made, such as blocks of completely landscaped terrain, mountains complete with trees and tunnels, perhaps supplied in sections or even modules, complete towns and cities, and so forth. These will be popular with model train enthusiasts whose interest is only in the trains, not in handcrafting an entire pike. Some of this ready-made scenery and landscaping is already beginning to appear on the market.

The principal advance to look forward to will be radio control. Each loco will have its own frequency. On the accompanying power pack, a selector switch will key into the loco you wish to control. That loco will then respond to the common throttle. The loco can be a modern *Metroliner* diesel or a vintage 1860 steamer. The authenticity of your carefully assembled pike might suffer slightly, however. Who ever saw a Civil War loco with a radio aerial extending from its cab or tender?

Even push-pull floor trains are changing from the early crude models that started the train hobby. Today many are powered by small batteries. Some make *chug-chug* sounds. One plays music when a small phonograph record is inserted in the rear of the loco. None uses tracks. But one has a unique arrangement: a special wire is laid across the floor in curves, even loops, and the battery-powered loco mysteriously follows the wire in its turns and twists. There are no cars following it because, apparently, cars don't have the ability to follow the wire as they do a track.

What the push-pull trains of tomorrow will be is anybody's guess.

17. TIPS,
TRICKS, AND GIMMICKS

1. MAKE YOUR PIKE UNIQUE: Although it may be no more than a simple circle, use two or more separate stations or freight depots (for a freight train) on different parts of the track. Give the stations eye-catching, tongue-twisting names. At least one such station certainly belongs on a siding. Then run your train on a schedule—after two revolutions of the track it stops at one station; after three more revolutions it stops at the second station, etc.

2. PROTECT SMALL PARTS: Loco and car kits usually contain a variety of small parts (screws, springs, etc.). As soon as you open the original box, put its tiny parts in an empty plastic pill bottle so you won't lose any of them, which is amazingly simple to do. When you're ready to work with them, spill them from their bottle into a cup or a muffin tray. A little screw can roll off a table quite easily.

3. DUST PROTECTOR: Dust can be one of your pike's worst enemies. The air in your room may seem to be dust-free, but it isn't. It may take a week or more before you notice it on your trains, buildings, and scenery, and then you have the job of getting rid of it. It gives colors a dull look, artificial, not realistic. When you've finished with your pike till your next free time period, cover it carefully with a plastic drop cloth or old sheet. Get someone to help you put it in place and take it off, with each of you holding opposite ends of the sheet and raising or lowering it carefully. If you try to do it yourself, you'll topple buildings and trees. Incidentally, if your loco picks up

dust through its belly and it reaches the motor, you'll be in for a complete disassembly and cleaning job.

4. STORING CARS AND LOCOS: If a car or loco is to be stored away indefinitely, first wrap it in Saran Wrap, the clear self-adhering plastic used for sandwiches and leftover foods. It protects cars from ·dust and moisture.

5. PASSENGER CAR SEATS: You can make seats for your passenger cars from Styrofoam. Make each in two pieces—the seat itself, then the seat back. The Styrofoam is easy to cut; your greatest problem will be cutting all of them to the same size. Paint them red or dark green before gluing them in place.

6. CAR LIGHTS: For realistic interior lighting of a passenger car, install a tiny "grain-of-wheat" bulb (a miniature bulb made especially for hobbyists) at one end of the roof's interior. The easiest way is to wire the bulb to a penlight battery hidden in the car. The roof must be removable, of course. With the bulb in place, glue a strip of Lucite along the roof's interior, running from the bulb. Before attaching the Lucite strip, with a file make a notch in it about every inch along its length. File the notches halfway through the strip. The Lucite will transmit the light through its length, but the sides of the notches will reflect some of the light downward, illuminating the seats. This will appear like a string of lights along the car's ceiling.

7. TRAYS FOR KITS: A clean aluminum plate with compartments, like the ones that come with TV dinners, is handy to hold kit parts during assembly. Put the large pieces in the large tray compartment, the other parts in smaller compartments. It will keep freight trucks from doing their favorite trick—rolling off the table.

8. MARKER LIGHTS: One of the modeler's toughest jobs is placing the tiny jewel (sold inexpensively by hobby shops and also included in locomotive kits) in a marker light of a loco or tender in the right position. A pair of tweezers helps, but the task is still a most delicate one. A small piece of soft modeling clay, available in art supply shops, will help. Place the jewel face-first on a small piece of this clay. Place glue on the recess of the marker, then press the back of the jewel, which is held in the clay, into the recess. It's easy to position it this way. Hold the clay and jewel in place a few minutes until the glue dries. Then the clay can be removed easily without disturbing the jewel.

9. ARTIFICIAL CANVAS: It's easy to make an old-time freight car or caboose, shed, or building look as though it has a canvas roof. First varnish the solid roof, then before it dries carefully spread on a single sheet of facial tissue, such as Kleenex. (Some tissues are doubled; be sure you separate the two pieces and use just the single piece.) When it's dry, trim it and paint it, and you'll have one of the prettiest pieces of miniature canvas you've ever seen.

10. REPLACING COUPLER SPRINGS: Plastic couplers are operated by the elasticity of the plastic; this, perhaps, is their greatest advantage. But metal couplers, such as Kadee, require a tiny spring to close the gripping jaw. And sometimes, during handling, this spring will pop off into oblivion. Realizing this possibility, Kadee includes a few extra springs in each envelope of couplers. Putting one of these springs in place requires extreme patience plus some manual dexterity. Here's the trick that helps. Coat the two prongs of a pair of tweezers with rubber cement to prevent slipping. (Don't close the tweezers; the cement is apt to lock them together.) This cement coating will prevent the spring from slipping away. Then insert one prong of the tweezers in the coil spring one loop from the end, and the other prong one loop from the other end. Now carefully compress the coiled spring, holding it steady with two fingers of the other hand, just in case. Put the spring in place; use another complete coupler as a reference. Open the tweezers and withdraw them carefully, and the job is done. The rubber cement on the ends can easily be coaxed to let go.

11. MODELER'S VISE: You'll find many uses for a small modeler's vise, an inexpensive item available at your hobby shop. A turn of its lever will anchor it solidly, by suction, to any smooth surface. Its jaws will hold a track while you shorten its rails with a razor saw or cut shorter sections of track, and they will hold small parts while you paint them. The vise will even hold the coupler when you're replacing its spring.

12. TRY KITBASHING: Take two or more kits (start with kits of buildings) and combine parts of each to make a building or house of your own design, cutting and trimming with an X-acto knife where necessary. Some modelers do it with freights, or even with diesel locos.

13. REMOVING PAINT SPOTS: If you accidentally get a spot or two of Floquil paint on a place where it doesn't belong, immediately

dip the end of a small, clean brush in Dio-sol and brush lightly on the spot. There won't be enough solvent to affect even styrene plastic and the brush will pick up the spot of paint. Not a trace will remain.

14. THINNING PAINT: For most paint jobs, the Floquil is used directly from its small bottle. When the cap is off the bottle, especially if it's for half an hour or so, some of the Dio-sol solvent will evaporate, thickening the paint slightly. To compensate for this loss, before replacing the cap on the paint bottle after use, add a few drops of Dio-sol.

15. STEEL STRAPS FOR FLATCARS: To simulate the steel bands used to tie loads such as lumber and logs to flatcars, use narrow strips of light, thin cellophane. Fasten the ends together beneath the car with Testor's glue. With some loads you can wrap the pieces together in a bundle, then "tie" with the cellophane strips. Finally, paint the strips black. If you know someone who still smokes cigarettes, you can save yourself the trouble of cutting the thin strips—use the thin ribbon of cellophane that tears off the top of the cigarette package wrapper. But paint it black. Instead of painting the strip with a brush, before fastening a strip to the load, dip it in the bottle of black paint and hang it over paper to drip dry. Before gluing the ends, scrape off some paint with your fingernail so the glue will hold to the plastic.

16. FLATCAR LOADS: For a load of pipes on a flatcar, use pieces of spaghetti, (uncooked, of course). Just snap them to reduce them to the length of the flatcar. For large pipes, use soda straws, cut to length. First dip each piece of spaghetti or straw in black paint and let dry before "tying" with plastic strips as explained in No. 15. A spool of wire, the spool ends painted black, can double on an HO flatcar for the large underground cables used by electric companies. So will wire wrapped around empty adhesive tape spools.

17. SUBSTITUTE FILE: If you don't have a regular file for removing flashing from cast metal parts of a loco before assembly, and for smoothing the edges of plastic building parts, use a steel fingernail file. The flashings are soft and will come off easily, and the scar can be removed by rubbing with light, firm pressure. Plastic parts should be braced tightly so they won't crack.

18. CAR WEIGHTS: Weighted freights and passenger cars will usually ride more smoothly. In a loco, added weight will increase

traction. Use lead fishing sinkers of appropriate sizes. Place them inside cars where they won't be seen. In a loco, there's usually room in the front of the boiler. But don't add too much weight. Freights that are too heavy, when left on a siding without a loco, will start rolling all by themselves; and locos can get too heavy for their limited power. Test after each weight is added.

19. BRILLIANT MARKER LIGHTS: Increase the shine of marker lights by giving the face of each jewel a dab of clear nail polish. Apply after the jewels have been glued in place. The polish will increase the light reflection from the jewel.

20. NAME PROTECTORS: The letters and names you have applied to your loco, tender, and cars can wear off if accidentally rubbed too hard with the fingers, sometimes very easily. Protect the lettering with a quick spray from a can of plastic spray, available at a stationery store. Don't apply too much; it's apt to shine artificially.

21. LOCO WHEEL CLEANER: Loco wheels can pick up an amazing amount of dirt from the rails, much more than that which clings to car wheels. In a loco this dirt can lessen electrical contact. To remove this dirt, place the loco on its back on a block of Styrofoam with a well cut in it to support the loco. Then run wires from your power pack and hold in place on the loco so the wheels will spin. While they're spinning, hold an ink eraser on the wheel and against the flange. A few seconds on each wheel should be sufficient. Nondriving wheels must be turned by hand.

22. TENDER COAL: Make your loco tender look as though it carries real coal by cutting a piece of foam plastic into the shape a load of coal should have, and gluing it in the tender. Then paint it with a weak solution of Elmer's glue (according to instructions for dilution on the bottle) and sprinkle some track ballast on it. Finally, paint the top and ballast black. Looks like honest coal.

23. CAR LOAD HOLDERS: To hold loose loads such as logs and lumber on a flatcar, run a cord around them and under the car; tie the ends of the cord to a spring to supply tension. Move the cord so the spring is below the car. The load will be held in place while the car moves, but can easily be removed by stretching the spring.

24. REMOVABLE LOADS: If your freight load is such that it must be glued together and to the car, first lay a sheet of brown paper

on the bottom of the car. Then when you want to remove the load, it will come out easily in one piece without damaging the car's finish.

25. CAR GRAFFITI: In the past decade, almost all prototype trains have acquired their share of graffiti, and now it has become almost a trademark of the railroad business. Keep in step with modern times by adding graffiti to your latest-style passenger cars and freights with fine-pointed grease pencils.

26. NEEDLE OILER: A needle can be used to deposit very small amounts of oil. Dip it in the bottle and withdraw it, being careful not to let it touch the sides of the bottle neck. Then touch the point to the spot you want to oil. Surface tension will draw off the oil clinging to the needle, and a very small amount will be placed where you want it.

MY SOURCES OF MATERIALS
AND INFORMATION

I. MANUFACTURERS AND THEIR SPECIALTIES

ALCO MODELS . . . *for locomotives and cars*
   P.O. Box 211, Port Jefferson, N.Y. 11777

AMERICA'S HOBBY CENTER . . . *for all products, mail order and discount*
   146 West 22nd Street, New York, N.Y. 10011

ATHEARN, INC. . . . . *for freights and freight kits*
   1510 West 135th Street, Gardena, Calif. 90249

ATLAS TOOL CO., INC. . . . *for tracks, cars, and locomotives*
   378 Florence Avenue, Hillside, N.J. 07205

BACHMANN BROS., INC. . . . *for all tracks and accessories except kits*
   1400 East Erie Avenue, Philadelphia, Pa. 19124

BOWSER MANUFACTURING CO. . . . *for locomotives*
   21 Howard Street, Mountoursville, Pa. 17754

CAMINO SCALE MODELS . . . *for building kits*
   P.O. Box 10666, Eugene, Ore. 97401

CAMPBELL SCALE MODELS . . . *for buildings, landscapes, and human and animal figures*
   P.O. Box 121, Tustin, Calif. 92680

COLOR-RITE SCENERY PRODUCTS . . . *for landscaping*
   2041 Winnetka Avenue North, Minneapolis, Minn. 55427

FLOQUIL-POLLY S COLOR CORP. . . . *for paint*
Route 30 North, Amsterdam, N.Y. 12010

KADEE QUALITY PRODUCTS CO. . . . *for couplers and N gauge products*
720 South Grape Street, Medford, Ore. 97501

KEMTRON CORP. . . . *for authentic details for locomotives and cars*
P.O. Box 360, Walnut, Calif. 91789

KEYSTONE LOCOMOTIVE WORKS . . . *for locomotives*
159 Wheatley Avenue, Northumberland, Pa. 17857

LIFE-LIKE PRODUCTS, INC. . . . *for train sets*
1600 Union Avenue, Baltimore, Md. 21211

LIONEL (FUNDIMENSIONS) . . . *for train sets*
Division General Mills Fun Group, Mount Clemens, Mich. 48045

MODEL DIE CASTING INC. . . . *for locomotives and car kits*
3811 West Rosecrans Avenue, Hawthorne, Calif. 90250

MODEL POWER (ROUNDHOUSE PRODUCTS) . . . *for train sets, locomotives, and buildings*
180 Smith Street, Farmingdale, N.Y. 11735

MODEL RECTIFIER CORP. (MRC) . . . *for power packs*
2500 Woodbridge Avenue, Edison, N.J. 08817

MOUNTAINS IN MINUTES . . '. *for landscaping*
I.S.L.E. Laboratories, Sylvania, Ohio 43560

PLASTRUCT, INC. . . . *for scratch building materials*
1161 Monterey Park Road, Monterey Park, Calif. 91754

REVELL INC. . . . *for landscaping*
4223 Glencoe Avenue, Venice, Calif. 90291

E. SUYDAM CO. . . . *for building kits*
P.O. Box 55, Duarte, Calif. 91010

TRU-SCALE MODELS, INC. . . . *for tracks and buildings*
P.O. Box 8157, Prairie Village, Kan. 66208

TYCO INDUSTRIES INC. . . . *for train sets*
540 Glen Avenue, Moorestown, N.J. 08057

WM. K. WALTHERS INC. . . . *for complete HO and N gauge catalogs*
5601 West Florist Avenue, Milwaukee, Wis. 53218

WOODLANDS SCENICS . . . *for landscaping*
   P.O. Box 266, Shawnee Mission, Kan. 66201
X-ACTO . . . *for modeling knife*
   45-35 Van Dam Street, Long Island City, N.Y. 11101

II. ASSOCIATIONS

NATIONAL MODEL RAILROAD ASSOCIATION (NMRA)
   P.O. Box 2186, Indianapolis, Ind. 46206
RAILROADIANA COLLECTORS ASSOCIATION
   405 Byron Avenue, Mobile, Ala. 36609

III. MONTHLY MAGAZINES

(SUBSCRIPTION, HOBBY SHOPS, NEWSSTANDS)

Model Railroader, Kalmbach Publishing Co.
   1027 North Seventh Street, Milwaukee, Wis. 53233
Railroad Model Craftsman, Carstens Publications
   P.O. Box 700, Newton, N.J. 07860
Railroad Modeler, Challenge Publications Inc.
   7950 Deering Avenue, Canoga Park, Calif. 91304

IV. BIBLIOGRAPHY

Botkin, B. A., and Harlow, Alvin F. *A Treasury of Railroad Folklore,*
   New York: Bonanza Books, 1953
Schleicher, Robert. *Model Railroading Handbook,*
   Radnor, Pa.: Chilton Book Co., 1975
Sutton, David. *The Complete Book of Model Railroading,*
   New York: Castle Books, 1964
Weiss, Harvey. *How To Run a Railroad,*
   New York: Crowell, 1977

INDEX

A

A & D Toy-Train Village and
  Railroad Museum, 17, 121
Accessories, 101–7; cassette tape
  recorder, 105–7; maintenance, 110,
  113–14; radio-controlled, 126;
  turntable, 84, 98, 103–5. *See also*
  names of accessories
AC current, 5, 51, 90, 91, 93, 113
Airbrush, 69
Alco (locomotive), 40
American (locomotive), 37
American Flyer trains, 17
America's Hobby Center, 32, 40
Amtrak, 75, 120
Architecture, *see* Buildings
Arnold, Adolf, 121
Articulated locomotives, 5, 38, 55
Athearn, Inc., 46
Atlantic (locomotive), 37
Atlas Tool Company, 52, 93, 96, 100
Automobile carriers, 42

B

Bachmann Brothers, 31, 32, 45, 61,
  63, 64, 76, 77, 93, 103, 123
Baggage cars, 42
Ballast, 5, 25, 54
Berkshire (locomotive), 37, 55

Billboard, 23, 101, 113, 123
Block system, 5, 93–94, 96, 120
Boxcars, 5, 42
Brass hat, 5
Buildings, 23–24, 54, 61–65, 71, 101;
  assembling, 63, 64; installing, 87;
  kits, 48–50, 61, 64; maintenance,
  113; painting and decorating,
  63–64, 66–70; weathering, 64, 70
Bullet, The (train set), 31

C

Caboose, 5, 31, 42, 44, 103
Campbell Scale Models, 48, 64;
  enginehouse kit, 105
Canvas, artificial, 132
Cars, *see* Rolling stock
Cassette tape recorder, 105–7
Cattle car, 5
CB (citizens band) transmitter, 126
Central Pacific Railroad, 13
Chattanooga Choo-Choo (train set),
  21
Chesapeake & Ohio Railroad, 84
Chicago World's Fair of 1933–34, 17
Circuit breaker, 5
Circus car, 47
Civil War, 13

Clockwork motor, 14, 15
Cog engine, 5, 35–36
Comet (train set), 45
Computerized train control, 126–27
Consolidation (locomotive), 37, 40, 48
Controller switch, 96
Control panel, 22–23, 98–100
Cornfield (head-on) collision, 6, 23, 120
Cost, 19, 20–21
Couplers, 6, 37, 44–45, 46–47, 105; replacing springs, 132
Cowcatcher, 6, 37
Crossover track, 6, 58, 59, 60
Curvature, track, 54–55, 56, 57
Curved turnouts, 57
Cylinders, 6

D
DC current, 6, 90, 91, 112–13
Dead (nonelectrified) track, 6, 23, 93–94, 96, 120
Decorating, *see* Painting and decorating
Derailments, avoiding, 58–60
Diesel locomotives, 6, 31, 32, 39–40, 41, 47, 128
Dio-sol paint thinner, 66, 67, 68, 70, 133
Drawbridges, 101
Dribbler (locomotive), 16
Driving wheels (drivers), 6
Dummy engine, 6
Dust protector, 130–31

E
Egypt (ancient), 2
Electrical power, 21–23; AC current, 5, 51, 90, 91, 93, 113; control panel, 22–23, 98–100; DC current, 6, 90, 91, 112–13; power pack, 7, 23, 29, 51, 90–91, 93, 96, 98, 112–13; safety of, 21–22; wiring, 22–23, 87, 90–100
Electricity, basic principles of, 51–52

EMD F-40 (locomotive), 40
EMD F-9 (locomotive), 31
Engineer's cap, 117
Enginehouses (roundhouses), 8, 103, 105, 113
E60CP (locomotive), 120

F
File, 133
First train, setting up, 27–80; architecture, 51, 61–65, 71; do-it-yourself kits, 46–50, 61–65; landscaping, 71–80; locomotive, 29, 35–41, 44, 46, 47, 48, 52, 55, 58; painting and decorating, 63–64, 66–70; rolling stock, 29, 42–45, 46–50, 58, 70; tracks, 29, 30, 51–60, 71, 79; train sets, 29–34
Flange, 6
Flatcars, 6, 42; load holders, 133, 134; loads for, 31, 133
"Flex-track" (flexible track), 6, 56
"Floor trains," 14, 15, 129
Floquil-Polly S Color Corp., 66–70; Glaze, 67; Instant Weathering, 64, 66, 69–70; paints, 64, 66, 80, 98, 133; RR19 Barrier, 68; stain, 70
Flywheel motor, 14
Freight depots, 130
Freight trains, 6, 42–44, 84, 94, 101, 119, 120, 130; in kits, 46–47
Frog, 6
F-3 Streamliner (locomotive), 40
Fudging, 6
Future, planning for, 125–29; computerized control, 126–27; high-speed trains, 127–28; radio control, 125–26, 129

G
Gapping, 6
Gauge sizes, 6; development of, 16–18
Gilbert Co., A. C., 17
Gimmicks, 130–35
Golden Spike ceremony, 13

Gondola, 44
GP-9 (locomotive), 40
GP-20 (locomotive), 40
Grab iron, 7
Grades, 71–72
Graffiti, 135
Grass, artificial, 76–77, 78–79

H

Heavy engines, 35
Highballing, 1, 7
High-speed trains, 127–28
Hills and mountains, making, 72–77, 87–88
Hog (pig), 7
HO gauge, 6, 17–18, 20, 33, 34, 87, 88, 118, 123, 124, 125; electrical current in, 51–52; kits, 48; landscaping, 25, 79; locomotive, 17, 18, 36, 40; rerailer track, 58; roadbed for, 86; track curvature, 54–55; train sets, 30–31
Homosote, 30, 33, 56, 64, 73, 74, 79, 86, 87, 98, 100
Hopper, 7, 31
How To Wire Your Model Railroad, 100
Hudson (locomotive), 37, 55
Humping, 7

I

Indianapolis Motor Speedway, 127
Instant Weathering paint, 64, 66, 69–70
Instruction booklet, 29
Ives Company, 15, 16

J

Joiners, *see* Rail joiners
Joy-Line key wind-up, 15

K

Kadee remote-control uncoupler, 45, 46–47, 105, 132
Kibri kits, 48
Kitbashing, 7, 132

Kits, 7, 46–50; buildings, 48–50, 61–65; enginehouse, 105; locomotive, 48, 109, 130; rolling stock, 46–47, 130; trays for, 131

L

Lakes, artificial, 77–78
Landscaping, 24–25, 71–80; artificial lakes and rivers, 77–78; grades, 71–72; maintenance, 113; making hills and mountains, 72–77, 87–88; roadbeds, 78–79; trees, 76, 77, 80; tunnels, 73, 74–75, 83; wall murals, 79–80
Layout Expander system, 32
Leading (pilot) truck, 7, 36, 37, 38
Light engines, 35
Lionel, 16, 17, 19, 60; accessories, 103
Live rail, 7
Live steamers, 15, 16
Locomotives, 21, 35–41, 44, 46, 47, 84, 96, 117, 120; added weight in, 133–34; articulated, 5, 38, 55; diesel, 6, 31, 32, 39–40, 41, 47, 128; historic, 14; HO gauge, 17, 18, 36, 40; kits, 48, 109, 130; maintenance, 108–10; motors in, 14, 52; N gauge, 36, 40; positioning on track, 58; power for, 90–91; radio-controlled, 126, 129; in return loop, 83, 96–97; smoking, 124; steam, 5, 15, 16, 32, 35, 36–38, 40–41, 48, 105, 110, 123; storing, 131; three types of, 35; in train set, 29; wheel cleaner, 134
Logging cars, 42

M

Magnetic uncoupler, 44–45, 46–47, 105, 132
Maintenance, 108–14; of accessories, 110, 113–14; landscaping and architecture, 113; locomotive, 108–10; power pack, 112–13; track, 110–12

Maintenance cars, 42
Marker lights, 131
Metroliner, 42, 119, 129
Mikado (locomotive), 37
Model Die Casting, Inc., 47, 48, 111
Modeler's vise, 132
Model Power Company, 40; accessories, 103; kits, 48
Model railroad clubs, 19, 20
Model Railroader (magazine), 40, 84
Model railroading: accessories, 101–7; beginning of, 13–18; building an empire, 2, 115–35; buildings, 23–24, 54, 61–65, 71, 101; and cats, 88–89; choosing rolling stock, 42–45; cost, 19, 20–21; do-it-yourself kits, 7, 46–50, 61–65, 105, 107, 109, 130; first train, 27–80; in the future, 125–29; installing tracks, 51–60, 83–89; landscaping, 24–25, 71–80; maintenance, 108–14; painting and decorating, 63–64, 66–70, 98, 113; perfecting your pike, 117–24; planning a pike, 81–114; present-day, 19–25; selecting a locomotive, 35–41; tips, tricks, and gimmicks for, 130–35; track layout, 83–89; train sets, 29–34; vocabulary, 5–9; wiring, 90–100; wonders of, 1–3
Model Rectifier Corporation (MRC), 32, 126
Mogul (locomotive), 37
Monorail, 125
Mountain (locomotive), 37
Mountains and hills, making, 72–77, 87–88
MOW, 7, 45

N
Name protectors, 134
Naming a pike, 117–18
National Model Railroad Association (NMRA), 19
Needle oiler, 135

New York Central Railroad, 41, 84, 117, 123
N gauge, 6, 17–18, 33, 34, 124, 125; electric current in, 52; landscaping, 79; locomotives, 36, 40; rerailer track, 58; roadbed for, 86; track curvature, 54–55; train sets, 30–31, 32
Northern (locomotive), 37, 55

O
Observation cars, 42
O gauge, 6, 16–18, 88; accessories, 103; electrical current in, 51–52; landscaping, 79; power pack, 90; roadbed for, 86; track, 17–18; train sets, 30–31
Ore cars, 42

P
Pacific (locomotive), 37, 40
Paint, thinning, 66, 67, 68, 70, 133
Painting and decorating, 63–64, 66–70, 98, 113
Painting Miniatures, 70
Paint spots, removing, 132–33
Passenger trains, 42, 45, 84, 94, 119, 120, 123; seats, 131; tickets for, 121–22
Perfecting your pike, 117–24; adding excitement, 122–24; making a schedule, 118–19; naming, 117–18; second engineer, 120; tickets, 121–22
Piddler (locomotive), 16
Pike, planning, 81–114; accessories, 101–7; definition, 7; for the future, 125–29; maintenance, 108–14; perfecting, 117–24; tips, tricks, and gimmicks, 130–35; track layout, 83–89; wiring, 87, 90–100; on wooden blocks, 103–5
Pilot (leading) truck, 7, 36, 37, 38
Plaster of Paris, 72
Polarity, reversing, 96, 97–98
Power pack, 7, 23, 51, 90–91, 93, 96,

98; maintenance, 112–13; in train set, 29
Prairie (locomotive), 37
Prototype, defined, 7
Push-pull floor trains, 14, 15, 129

R
Radio control, 125–26; locomotive, 126, 129
Rail Blazer (train set), 31
Rail joiners, 7, 52, 56, 60, 91; maintenance, 111–12; plastic, 93–94
Railroad empire, 2, 115–35; perfecting your pike, 117–24; planning for the future, 125–29; tips, tricks, and gimmicks, 130–35
Ratlum Mountain Railroad, 117
Ready-track, 54
Rectifier, 7
Reefers (refrigerator cars), 7, 31, 42
Removable loads, 134–35
Rerailer track, 7, 58, 79, 91
Return loop, 8, 83; wiring, 96–97
Rivers, artificial, 77–78
Roadbeds, 8, 78–79; perfecting, 86–87; variations in, 127
Rock Island Railroad, 41
Rolling stock, 8, 42–45; couplers, 37, 44–45, 46–47, 105; graffiti on, 135; in kits, 46–47, 130; lights in, 131; load holders, 133, 134; positioning on track, 58; storing, 131; in train sets, 29; weathering, 44, 70; weights for, 133–34; for younger beginners, 42. *See also* names of cars
Roundhouse Products, 47, 48
Roundhouses (enginehouses), 8, 103, 105, 113

S
Santa Fe Railroad, 41
Schedule, making, 118–19
Schienenzeppelin (high-speed train), 123
Scratch building, 8

Sectional track, 52–54; advantage of, 54
S gauge, 17
Shifter (locomotive), 40
Shoe, 8
Short circuit, 5, 8, 51, 91–93, 96
Siding, 8, 84, 120; insulated, 94
Sleeper cars, 42
Slip switch, 8, 57–58
Smithsonian Institution, 15
Smoking locomotives, 124
Spurs, 8, 84
Steam locomotives, 5, 15, 16, 32, 36–38, 40–41, 105, 110, 123; kits, 48; three types of, 35
Steam whistle, 23, 101, 113, 123
Stock cars, 42
String, 8
Striping wheel, 68
Styrene plastic, 67–68
Suydam kits, 48
Switchers, 8, 35, 40
Swiveling trucks, 55
SW-1 (locomotive), 40

T
Tank car, 42, 46
Tech II power pack, 91
Tenders, 8, 37, 40, 48, 117, 134
Terminal board, 93
Terminal track, 8, 57, 91
Testor's glue, 50
Tickets, 121–22
Ties, 8
Tips, 130–35
Track joiners, *see* Rail joiners
Tracks, 51–60; crossovers, 58, 59, 60; curvature of, 54–55, 56, 57; dead (nonelectrified), 6, 23, 93–94, 96, 120; layout, 83–89; maintenance, 110–12; mounting, 30; O gauge, 17–18; rerailer, 58, 79, 91; terminal, 57, 91; in train set, 29; turnouts, 19, 22, 54, 56–58, 60, 71, 83–84, 86, 93, 94, 96, 110, 120,

127; types of, 52–54, 56; warnings about, 59–60. *See also* Wiring
Trailing (rear) truck, 36, 37
Train set, 8, 29–34; buying, 32–33; contents of, 29; cost of, 31–32; selecting a gauge, 30–31
Transcontinental railroad, 13
Trees, artificial, 76, 77, 80
Tricks, 130–35
Tru-Track, 52–54
TT (table top) gauge, 17
Tunnels, 73, 74–75, 83
Turnaround methods, 96–98
Turnouts (switches), 19, 22, 54, 56–58, 60, 71, 83–84, 94, 96, 110, 120, 127; remote, 93; roadbed under, 86
Turntable, 84, 98, 103–5
Tyco Industries, 21, 23, 31–32, 40, 48, 93, 113, 123; accessories, 101

U
Union Pacific Railroad, 13, 84
U. S. Patent Office, 15

V
Vista-dome cars, 42

Vocabulary for model railroaders, 5–9

W
Wall murals, 79–80
Weathering, 44, 64, 66, 69–70
Whistle, 23, 101, 113, 123
Wilkins Co., 15
Wiring, 87, 90–100; block system, 5, 93–94, 96, 120; control panel, 22–23, 98–100; power pack, 7, 23, 29, 51, 90–91, 93, 96, 98, 112–13; for a return loop, 96–97; reversing polarity, 96, 97–98; short circuit, 5, 8, 51, 91–93, 96; terminal board, 93
World War II, 2, 17–18
Wye turnarounds, 60, 97, 99–100

X
X-acto knife, 86, 99

Z
ZAP glue, 50

ABOUT THE AUTHOR

Until several years ago, Gil Paust was editor in chief of a national magazine. He has had hundreds of his own stories published in addition to a dozen books. He has B.A. and M.A. degrees from Columbia University, and has taught in high school and college. He has also been an aircraft pilot and an instructor of Air Force cadets. A native of New York State, Gil Paust and his wife, Anne, live in Westchester County, New York, and their hideaway on Ratlum Mountain, Connecticut.